W9-DBM-123

GOVERNMENT DOCUMENTS LIBRARIANSHIP

A Guide for the Neo-Depository Era

Lisa A. Ennis

Information Today, Inc.
Medford, New Jersey

First printing, 2007

Government Documents Librarianship: A Guide for the Neo-Depository Era

Copyright © 2007 by Lisa A. Ennis

Publisher's Note: The editor and publisher have taken care in preparation of this book but make no expressed or implied warranty of any kind and assume no responsibility for errors or omissions. No liability is assumed for incidental or consequential damages in connection with or arising out of the use of the information or programs contained herein.

Many of the designations used by manufacturers and sellers to distinguish their products are claimed as trademarks. Where those designations appear in this book and Information Today, Inc. was aware of a trademark claim, the designations have been printed with initial capital letters.

Library of Congress Cataloging-in-Publication Data

Ennis, Lisa A., 1969-
  Government documents librarianship : a guide for the neo-depository era / Lisa A. Ennis.
    p. cm.
  Includes bibliographical references and index.
  ISBN-13: 978-1-57387-270-6
    1. Documents libraries--United States--Administration. 2. Libraries--United States--Special collections--Government publications. 3. Government publications--United States--Handbooks, manuals, etc. 4. Depository libraries--United States--Administration. 5. Documents librarians--United States. 6. United States. Government Printing Office. 7. Federal Depository Library Program. I. Title.
  Z688.G6E56 2007
  025.17'34--dc22

                                                                    2007017086

President and CEO: Thomas H. Hogan, Sr.
Editor-in-Chief and Publisher: John B. Bryans
Managing Editor: Amy M. Reeve
VP Graphics and Production: M. Heide Dengler
Book Designer: Kara Mia Jalkowski
Cover Designer: Dana Kruse
Indexer: Beth Palmer

To find out about other great books from Information Today, Inc. or to request a free catalog, visit books.infotoday.com

For Nicole

Contents

CHAPTER 5

CHAPTER 6

CHAPTER 7

CHAPTER 8

Foreword

Since 1789, the U.S. Government has been "Keeping America Informed" by providing the public with unrestricted, no-fee access to federal government information. The Government Printing Office (GPO) is responsible for the printing of documents produced by federal agencies, while the GPO's Federal Depository Library Program (FDLP) is responsible for the distribution of documents in all formats to the approximately 1,200 designated federal depository libraries that exist in the country today.

Each depository library receives the documents it selects at no charge from the FDLP, though the documents remain the property of the U.S. Government. In its role of custodian, the depository library is required to receive, process, house, maintain, preserve, and provide access to the documents and to follow federal laws, rules, and regulations in doing so.

To ensure FDLP requirements are being met, the GPO has an inspection process in place, and, in late 1998 and early 1999, each of the 27 depository libraries in Georgia was required by the GPO to complete a self-study. The GPO reviewed the self-studies and, for a variety of reasons, decided to send an inspector to visit 17 libraries.

Following the inspections, four Georgia depository libraries were placed on probation by the GPO, including the Ina Dillard Russell Library at Georgia College & State University (GC&SU). In an April 2000 report, a GPO inspector found GC&SU to be noncompliant in five of the seven categories reviewed during the inspection visit. In the summary report, the inspector recommended that the library director decide whether to withdraw from the FDLP or to remain a depository and take the necessary actions to remove its probationary status.

After many meetings and discussions with library faculty and staff as well as the college faculty and administration, GC&SU decided to work towards FDLP compliance in order to remain in the program.

In December 2002, GC&SU was reinspected. This time, in each of the five noncompliant categories identified in the 2000 inspection report, the library earned a compliant rating. The GPO inspector reported that the amount of work and effort applied to improving this depository library was readily apparent throughout the reinspection visit. And that, "To use a trite phrase, it was as different as night and day!"

What were the factors that contributed to the remarkable turn-around in this depository library? Clearly the support of the university and library administrations was one; another was the dedication and hard work of the faculty and staff of the Ina Dillard Russell Library at GC&SU.

And then there was the librarian who volunteered to assume the responsibilities for the government documents collection, who stepped up to organize the repair effort that led to reinspection and put an end to the library's probationary status in the FDLP.

Lisa Ennis admits that she likes to volunteer for projects (big or small), that she enjoys puzzles and gets a kick out of fixing things. She's also the first to admit that, prior to volunteering to help turn around GC&SU's depository library, she had limited experience with government documents. (She admitted as much at the time.) In order to prepare for her new responsibilities, Lisa began an exhaustive search for information about government documents librarianship. She soon learned that there was much more information available about *accessing and using* federal government information resources than there was about *managing* a government documents collection.

During my 27 years of experience working with depository libraries and government documents librarians, I had never encountered a situation like the one that occurred at GC&SU. However, I am aware of librarians who have had documents responsibilities foisted upon them under circumstances that provided little, if any, introduction to or training in government documents. More than a few librarians have been asked to take responsibility for their institution's government documents collections on top of their regular duties. In many such instances, training by an experienced government documents librarian or staff member may not be available and the only option is to learn on the job.

For librarians in these situations, and for others who would like to learn more about managing a federal depository library or government documents collection, this book will be invaluable. While not intended as a step-by-step guide to managing each and every federal depository library, it provides a good introduction to the GPO, the FDLP, and government documents librarianship. Perhaps its greatest value lies in the fact that is based on the firsthand experience of a librarian who successfully took over the responsibilities for managing a government documents collection under difficult circumstances, only to discover that she loved the work.

—Susan Copony Field
U.S. Regional Depository Librarian
University of Georgia Libraries

Acknowledgments

As always there are too many people to acknowledge, and no doubt many of you will cash in your favors shortly. You all know who you are. I'd like to particularly thank the 2002 faculty and staff of the Ina Dillard Russell Library at Georgia College & State University. Without their dedication and hard work, we'd have never passed reinspection. Special thanks to Michael Aldrich, Government Documents Librarian at the Ingram Sullivan Library at the University of West Georgia, and Susan Field, Regional Depository Librarian at the University of Georgia, for their unending patience and guidance. I'd also like to thank the faculty and staff of the Lister Hill Library of the Health Sciences at the University of Alabama at Birmingham for their support and encouragement in this project. Special thanks to the reference department for putting up with me during the process!

Introduction:
What's Going On Here?

What This Book Is and Is Not

Sometimes knowing what something is not is more important than knowing what it is. This book is not a step-by-step guide to running a federal depository library collection. Even if I could give you step-by step-instructions, all the rules and questions would change by the time the ink hit the paper. Besides, step-by step-instructions are linear and don't leave much room for your own personality and creativity. While keeping these limitations in mind, it *is* my intention to present a useful guide. If I'm successful, this book will show you multiple ways of getting to where you need to be and inspire you to figure out your own new ways to get places. Along the way, I'll explain what the Federal Depository Library Program (FDLP) requires you to do as a depository librarian, offer suggestions and advice, and touch upon various topics of interest.

I should also point out that this book isn't about *using* government resources but about *managing* them within a depository library. There are other books that can help you learn to use Government Printing Office (GPO) publications. I've included a lengthy list of recommended resources in Appendix A, but the standard text is Joe Morehead's *Introduction to United States Government Information Sources* (sixth edition, 1999) and Judith Schiek Robinson's *Tapping the Government Grapevine: The User-Friendly Guide to U.S. Government Information Sources* (1988). Although both books are older, they remain important resources for government information professionals.

Government documents, the GPO, and the FDLP are experiencing and will continue to experience a tremendous amount of change. As the GPO and FDLP move to a more electronic environment, their roles will continue to evolve as will the role of government documents librarians. Many question if the FDLP and documents librarians are needed in the electronic environment. The answer is a resounding "Yes!" We need the FDLP and government documents librarians today more than ever.

Why Me?

A "Chihuahua in a Rottweiler world" is how I described myself at the 2003 Federal Depository Library Conference in Reno, Nevada. I tend to volunteer for things without much thought or realization as to the size of the project or problem. Much like a small dog, I'll take on just about anything, whether it is the size of a Rottweiler or not. So, when my library needed someone to coordinate the government documents collection, I volunteered—even though the collection was on probation, noncompliant in five of the seven areas evaluated by the GPO, and there was less than a year before a reinspection. As I told my supervisor, I love a good puzzle and I love to fix things. With nothing to lose, the library administration let me take a swing at repairing the collection. Turned completely loose to do what I believed needed to be done, I tried all the management stuff I'd always wanted to try and took a crash course in government documents librarianship. In the end, we came out compliant in all seven areas!

Organizational Matters

This book is organized into eight chapters. The first four examine government documents in a broad general way. Chapter 1, "Government Documents Librarianship," is an overview of what the title means and what it takes to be a documents librarian. Chapter 2, "GPO and FDLP History," is a sketch of the rich history of both organizations, while Chapter 3, "The Modern GPO and FDLP," takes a look at where they are today. Finally, Chapter 4, "FDLP Requirements," is an examination of what is required of the modern depository library. The last four chapters look at more specific areas of government documents. Chapter 5, "Networking and Training," explains and gives advice on all the various training opportunities for documents librarians as well as networking strategies. Chapter 6, "Managing and Administering," offers an examination of the managerial and administrative issues concerning documents, and Chapter 7, "Public Services Issues," covers the public services aspects of documents, including reference, instruction, and promotion. Finally, Chapter 8, "Technical Services Issues," covers all of the things that go on behind the scenes such as cataloging and processing.

Moving Forward

I loved being a documents librarian. The experience was simply one of the highlights of my career. In the process of writing this book, the editors would ask if I thought this or that was too "over the top" or did I "really feel that way." Maybe I did have a little too much fun creating my signage, and maybe I did get a little too excited about cataloging documents myself. Looking back, though, I did have a blast and I hope I made it fun for all my co-workers, too. And I hope this book is fun, too, whether you are in school just getting started, a veteran librarian looking for a new challenge, or someone who has just inherited a government documents collection. There are so many opportunities for information professionals today; I encourage you to grab them with enthusiasm. I invite you to write me with comments and suggestions (e-mail me at lennis@uab.edu). I'd love to hear from you!

CHAPTER 1

Government Documents Librarianship: The Sky's the Limit

In my experience, very few librarians plan to become government documents librarians, and the ones who do generally come from public services areas. Once you become a "documents person," however, you are one for life, even if you move on to other niches or jobs. As one retired government documents librarian wrote, "Many of us did not so much choose documents as a profession so much as we were chosen—and ultimately possessed—by it."[1] That is certainly what happened to me.

The little research on government documents librarians that exists mirrors my experience. In 1989, for instance, Barbara Cross and John Richardson conducted a survey which showed that out of 275 respondents, 75 percent "… did not plan on a career in government information and did not start out in government information …"; of those 75 percent, 31 percent worked in reference first, followed by 11 percent who were catalogers before becoming documents librarians.[2] In 2002, Zheng Ye (Lan) Yang found in her survey of 244 respondents that 62 percent began their careers in other areas of librarianship, with reference again leading the pack at almost 49 percent.[3]

Why don't librarians see government documents as a career path? Could it be that we librarians are to blame? Consider what Judith Schiek Robinson says in her book *Tapping the Government Grapevine*, in which she compares government documents to tomatoes. She explains that prior to 1820 tomatoes were shunned because they were thought to be poisonous, until one day someone ate a whole basket of them in front of a crowd. Schiek wrote, "Government publications are a lot like tomatoes. To this day their potential remains shrouded not by one misconception, but by many. Among the uninitiated librarians they enjoy a mystique that is fueled by unfamiliarity."[4] If we as librarians do not promote all facets of librarianship, then we have only ourselves to blame when those career paths fade and die. We must be our own biggest fans for all aspects of librarianship. So, with all that said, why should you or anyone else pursue a career as a government documents librarian?

First of all, this is an excellent time to be a librarian of any variety. I might have on rose-colored glasses, but to me, the opportunities and advantages of being an information professional in today's world are limitless. Librarians can go anywhere and do anything we set our minds to do. Government documents librarianship, however, offers some unique opportunities that are hard to find in other areas of librarianship and can be a fantastic training ground for branching off into any number of directions.

Before I begin to describe all the positives of being a government documents librarian, let me warn you that I'm a firm believer in the old adages "you get back only what you put in" and "the experience is as only as good as you make it." I never worked so hard or so fast as I did when I was a documents librarian. Do not expect any of the benefits I am about to discuss to fall into your lap. Documents librarianship will present you with many opportunities, but it's up to you to make the most of them. This means that you will have to work hard and take a risk every now and again.

Boundless Opportunities for the Fearless

So often in life things are both positive and negative, and government documents librarianship is no different. Something I see as a wonderful positive may be seen by another as horribly negative. Both perspective and individual circumstances come into play, but overall, I hope the following examples serve to demonstrate the broad range of possibilities and opportunities that a government documents librarian position offers.

First, being a depository coordinator allows you to participate in all facets of library operations. When I became depository coordinator, I suddenly found myself responsible for all aspects of the government documents collection. I was basically running a library within a library. I moved beyond my Instruction and Reference department into every other department and unit in the library, from processing to interlibrary loan to systems. While this may seem daunting, I loved it. I learned all about collection development, technical services, circulation, and, my favorite, cataloging. My knowledge of how the whole library operated grew. While not all depository librarians are as involved in other departments as I was, the opportunity is definitely there if you want to take advantage of it.

Also, by managing the collection, you get that all important and ever elusive management experience. As a depository librarian, you have oversight of all depository functions, and you generally will have at least one staff member who reports to you; I had one library associate and a student worker. So, not only do you get both administrative and supervisory experience, you also acquire experience in something that is much harder to accomplish—cross-departmental cooperation. Since managing the government documents collection requires all library departments to work together, you learn how to persuade people to do what you need them to do even though you have no authority over them or their areas. Much more on management is included in Chapter 6, "Managing and Administering."

This broad range of experiences is also an excellent way to gain the experience needed to advance your career. Managing an entire collection, directly supervising staff, and fostering teamwork among departments provides you with the necessary skills to become any sort of administrator you desire. I even got a little experience with the library budget. While I didn't move into management, I did move into another specialty: medical librarianship. Working with government documents, as well as volunteering to work as the School of Health Sciences liaison at my medium-sized public university, gave me the experience with PubMed, the National Library of Medicine, and U.S. Department of Health and Human Services resources that I needed to become a medical librarian at a major research university even though all my academic work had been in history.

Working in government documents also gives you the chance to be *the* expert for a facet of librarianship many consider to be difficult to master. For instance, when Walter Newsome, a retired government documents librarian from the University of Virginia, was assigned to the government documents department as a library school student, he found himself in "the domain of a small, energetic, extremely charming sorceress and all-round information wizard referred to in hushed, reverential tones as THE Documents Librarian."[5] I have definitely found this to be true. Documents, much as Robinson described them, have a reputation among other librarians as being different, convoluted, and hard to navigate. But, while documents are different, they hardly require the skills of a master cryptographer to decipher. By achieving fluency in a special field within the larger realm of librarianship, you show creativity, initiative, flexibility, and intelligence. The belief is that if you can "do documents," you can do anything!

Another benefit to belonging to the government documents world is the government documents community. The people who work in government documents are among the friendliest and most knowledgeable folks you'll ever meet. When I became documents coordinator of a collection on probation with less than a year to prepare for reinspection, I needed help. I don't know what I would have done without the network of documents librarians that exists in Georgia and all over the country. No matter what I needed, my new colleagues were always patient and kind. Never once was I made to feel silly.

Being a documents librarian is almost like belonging to a special club full of people who share the same experiences, problems, issues, and appreciation for government information resources. No matter where I went, if that library had a documents librarian, I had an immediate contact and ally. This close network can also prove to be a fantastic source of support. When I went up for tenure, for instance, the best letters of recommendation I received were from documents librarians who were familiar with me and my work.

Another interesting perk of being a documents specialist is that since it has such a reputation for being a difficult area to work in, the opportunities for publishing and presenting are abundant. If you work in a library that requires you to publish and present, government documents offers a whole host of possibilities for practically any library conference or publication, not just those dedicated solely to government resources. In fact, I even got invited to publish and present at a national conference because of my work with documents. Quite a boon for a librarian with promotion and tenure requirements!

Another aspect of documents librarianship I really enjoyed was getting to work with resources covering all kinds of topics and in a variety of formats. If, like me, you have a short attention span, government documents provides you with a seemingly endless supply of different kinds of materials that cover a wide range of topics. If I got tired of working with Department of Education materials, for instance, I could put those materials aside and work with Census resources, Department of Defense history materials, or U.S. Geological Survey maps. There always seemed to be a chunk of materials to match any mood.

I also enjoyed the challenge of being among the first to work with emerging technologies. Government agencies are usually among the first to use a new technology, so as a government documents librarian, you hear about and get to use these technologies first. If you are interested in technology and its application in libraries, government documents librarianship can put you on the "bleeding edge."

The American Library Association (ALA) Government Documents Round Table (GODORT) has pulled together a list of e-competencies, which are divided into three tiers: "E-Competencies That Every Depository Librarian Should Have"; "Skills Which At Least One Depository Staff Member/Librarian Must Have"; and "Skills Which Are Very Helpful to Have, Especially in a Depository Library Serving Clientele Performing Research."[6] While all the competencies together create a pretty formidable list, the ones in Tier I, "E-Competencies That Every Depository Librarian Should Have," are pretty basic for all librarians these days and include things such as competency with the Windows operating system, browsers, file formats, e-mail, and electronic catalogs.[7] Don't let any list of skills scare you, though. Learning as you go is perfectly acceptable!

Government Documents Librarian Without a Depository

Even if you do not work in a Federal Depository Library (FDL), you can become a government information specialist and your library can still offer access to government information. In fact, if you choose to pursue government information as a specialty, you can take advantage of all the previously mentioned opportunities. The prevalence and proliferation of electronic government publications and portals means that any librarian anywhere, as long as he or she has Internet access, can learn to become a government documents professional. So, if you are interested in government documents, do not let your library's lack of depository status hinder you.

In a 2005 presentation for the Joint Spring Meeting of the College and University Section and Technical Services Round Table of the Nebraska Library Association, James Shaw from the University of

Nebraska at Omaha (UNO) explained how and why his library downloads MARC records of government publications for inclusion in its library catalog. While UNO is a depository library, the important thing here is that any library can download MARC records for electronic government publications.

According to Shaw, cataloging electronic government resources is a worthwhile pursuit for a number of reasons. For one, it transforms the library's catalog into a gateway to government information. The catalog also does a better job of directing users to a specific resource than Internet search engines do, and it can link both print and electronic resources together, creating a complete record of the information available. Since most government resources are free, the library catalog directs users to full text information above and beyond library paid subscriptions. Another important aspect of cataloging online government resources is the ability to provide quick and accurate access to current "hot topics." As Shaw explains, the online version of the 9/11 Commission reports was posted prior to publication of the print version, and libraries of all kinds downloaded the record for the electronic version almost immediately.[8] We'll look more closely at cataloging in Chapter 8, "Technical Services Issues."

While Shaw does work in a FDL, Diann Weatherly of the Mervyn H. Sterne Library at the University of Alabama at Birmingham (UAB) does not. In her 1996 article, "A U.S. Government Publications Collection in a Non-Depository Library: A Case Study," Weatherly describes in detail how the Sterne Library built a government documents collection without belonging to the Federal Depository Library Program (FDLP). Weatherly's case study provides librarians with an interest in government information with a fantastic resource on how to build a collection without being a depository library. Importantly, as UAB's government document collection began before the 1995 "Electronic Federal Depository Library Program" was announced, the collection consisted of print and microfiche materials the Sterne Library purchased. As more and more government information is published on the Internet, any library can build and maintain an electronic collection of government resources.

Conclusion

While any career in librarianship is unlikely to lead to a life of fame and fortune, government documents librarianship offers creative and energetic librarians an opportunity to gain a wealth of experience in a variety of settings. The breadth and depth of government documents work is one of the most rewarding and enriching aspects of the specialty. So, no matter what kind of library you are employed in, finding a niche in government information is always possible. The most important advice I can give is that if you are interested in working with government information, just get started. You can begin to test the waters by creating a Web page or a handout on how to download tax forms or how to find health statistics. All you really need to succeed as a government documents librarian are a willingness to learn new things, an interest in technology, a commitment to providing government information to all, and a moderately sized stubborn streak.

From the Trenches

- If you are in school, take a government documents class if you can; if you can't or have already graduated, don't sweat it. On-the-job training is still the best way to learn.

- Explore all your possibilities and opportunities.

- If you aren't in an FDL but want to be, take a look at government documents job advertisements to get an idea of what you need to work on to apply for those jobs.

- Beef up your technology skills whenever and wherever you can.

- Ask other documents people for advice and help.

Endnotes

1. Barbara Kile, Ridley R. Kessler, Jr., and Walter Newsome, "Experience Speaks: Thoughts on Documents Librarianship," *DttP: Documents to the People* 32 (1), 15.

2. Barbara Marston Cross and John Richardson Jr., "The Educational Preparation of Government Information Specialists," *Journal of Education for Library and Information Science*, 36.

3. Zheng Ye (Lan) Yang, "An Assessment of Education and Training Needs for Government Documents Librarians in the United States," *Journal of Government Information* 28, 430.

4. Judith Schiek Robinson, *Tapping the Government Grapevine: The User-Friendly Guide to U.S. Government Information Sources* (Phoenix, AZ: Oryx Press, 1988), v.

5. Kile, Kessler, and Newsome, "Experience Speaks," 15.

6. "GODORT Government Information Technology Committee E-competencies." Available online at www.ala.org/ala/godort/godortcommunities/gitco/ecomps.htm.

7. "GODORT"

8. James T. Shaw, *How to Be a Depository Library Without Being a Depository Library: Adding Records for Electronic Government Documents to Our Catalog*, Joint Spring Meeting of the College and University Section and Technical Services Round Table of the Nebraska Library Association, Doane College, Crete, Nebraska, 2005.

CHAPTER 2

GPO and FDLP History: A Look Back Before Moving Forward

Both the Government Printing Office (GPO) and the Federal Depository Library Program (FDLP) have long, rich, and fascinating histories. While recounting them in detail is beyond the scope of this book, a bit of background is helpful in understanding the current directions of these entities. Throughout their histories, the GPO and the FDLP have navigated the rocky waters of national and world events, yet survived to carry forth their goals of keeping America informed. A look at where they have been will hopefully serve as inspiration for where we can take both the GPO and FDLP in this brave new digital world.

The Government Printing Office: A Little History

The GPO opened for business on March 4, 1861, the very same day that Abraham Lincoln was inaugurated as the 16th President of the United States. The building was constructed on H Street at North Capitol in a neighborhood known as the "Swampoodle" (because of the frequent overflow from the nearby Tiber Creek). The building was erected across the street from an infamous saloon that sold whiskey shots for 8 cents each.[1] Created by the Printing Act of June 23, 1860, the GPO replaced the expensive and sometimes corrupt system of contract printers that the federal government had used since 1789.[2] The purpose of the GPO was to make the work of the American government available to the public in a timely, efficient, and accurate manner. To undertake this monumental task, the GPO, which was headed by a Superintendent of Public Printing, employed 350 people in a new four-story building. The building's machinery was powered by steam and gas fixtures were used for lighting. Documents were delivered by horse and buggy.[3]

During the Civil War, GPO employees armed themselves to help defend Washington, D.C., from Confederate General Jubal Early's invading force camped just five miles from the city. Some employees were even part of the Interior Department's own military regiment. The regiment drilled, received military instruction, and guarded the GPO building every night. While Union General Ulysses Grant engaged Early, the GPO employees stood defensive posts, ready to defend both their building and their country. Once Grant had defeated Early, the workers returned to their jobs.[4]

Though the GPO was established in 1861, the position of Superintendent of Documents was not created until eight years later. The position was responsible for distributing documents to the various depository libraries and was initially a part of the Department of the Interior. In 1895, the position of Superintendent of Documents was transferred from the Department of the Interior to the GPO, and the job also assumed the additional duties of both the bibliographic control and the sale of government publications. To help with the issue of bibliographic control, Superintendent of Documents Francis A. Crandall hired librarian Adelaide Rosalie Hasse from the Los Angles Public Library. In an effort to organize and classify the collection, Hasse developed the beginnings of the SuDoc classification system still in use today.[5]

By 1873, just 13 years after it was established, the GPO was responsible for all the printing needs of all three branches of the federal government, as well as the huge task of printing all the proceedings and debates of Congress in the *Congressional Record*, which replaced the privately printed *Congressional Globe*. At the urging of the Librarian of Congress, Herbert Putnam, the GPO also established a unit at the Library of Congress. This unit was charged with producing the library's card catalog as well as binding, repairing, and restoring the library's collection.[6]

Since its inception, the GPO has implemented a number of new technologies. In 1866, for instance, the GPO bought the latest and greatest in printing technology: the Bullock Perfecting Press. This new press was the first automatic, reel-fed rotary press using stereotype plates, and it printed on both sides of the paper. The Bullock Press could print on the front and back of 10,000 sheets of paper each hour. In 1878, the GPO contracted to purchase three Two-Revolution

Cylinder Presses by Cottrell & Babcock. These new presses were so fast and efficient that two of them did the work of 12 of the older Adams presses and required the attention of fewer employees.[7] Throughout its long history, the GPO embraced change and technology, from electricity to automobiles.

As the agency grew, the GPO also used a variety of new and old methods to improve its buildings. In particular, Sterling Rounds made a huge impact as Public Printer from 1882 to 1886. In addition to creating a system for inspecting paper before paying for it, attacking patronage in hiring practices, and cleaning and renovating the entire building, Rounds paid very close attention to employee safety. He replaced old, small water lines with new larger ones. With fire always a threat, Rounds supplemented the iron fire escapes with canvas chutes for the upper floors, created a water bucket trolley system that completely surrounded the building's fourth floor, and installed fire hoses on each floor. He even stored bows and arrows at strategic locations so that ropes could be shot to people trapped in a fire.[8]

At the turn of the century, the *Washington Times* declared the GPO to be the "World's Greatest Printing Office."[9] The GPO got to demonstrate this greatness during both World War I and World War II. These two wars had a tremendous influence on the GPO and, conversely, the GPO had a huge impact on the war efforts. During World War I, the GPO printed everything from military manuals, Liberty Bond posters, and confidential materials to bulletins on home economics. Usually, millions of copies of a variety of different items were printed and delivered in just a few days. By 1918, the GPO employed 5,307 people who worked around the clock in three eight-hour shifts to meet the increased wartime demand.[10]

The situation was much the same during World War II, when the GPO again worked around the clock to meet demand. The GPO also supported its employees serving in the armed forces. For instance, the GPO sent each service member a Christmas care package consisting of items such as books, pencils, candy, soap, peanuts, and other personal items. Service members also received inspiration from Augustus "Gus" Giegengack, the Public Printer, in the form of a 1944 Christmas card, telling them "... you have seen the imprint of the Government Printing Office in all stages of the fight from the Training Manuals in camp to the [maps on] bombing tables used over Berlin and Tokyo. Look for the imprint on all your printed material."[11] In return, the GPO received letters back from service people, often with examples of how they had used government publications throughout the war.[12]

Two of the most striking examples of the GPO's efficiency and renown also come from the World War II time period. The day after President Franklin Delano Roosevelt (FDR) died on April 12, 1945, the GPO was given a rush order for 225,000 copies of "General Order 29" announcing FDR's death. The GPO received the request at 11:30 A.M. Within five hours, proofs were set, 64 plates were processed, and the copies were printed, bound, and delivered.[13] Also that same year, the GPO assumed responsibility for the printing needs of the international assembly charged with establishing the United Nations (UN). The 372-page UN Charter was handset in five different languages, including Russian and Chinese; the GPO met the signing deadline, although six signature copies had a missing Chinese character added in by hand.[14]

During the 1950s, the GPO once again geared up to deal with wartime printing demands as the situation in Korea continued to escalate. The 1952 presidential election also had an interesting effect on the GPO and Public Printer Raymond Blattenberger. Dwight D. Eisenhower was the first Republican president in two decades, so when he appointed Blattenberger as Public Printer, people expected Blattenberger to fire all the Democrats and replace them with Republicans. Blattenberger, however, had other plans and even refused to fire the Democrat Deputy Public Printer, Philip L. Cole. Blattenberger's refusal to participate in the political maneuverings of his party made him some powerful enemies. Both he and Cole were even questioned by Senator Joseph McCarthy's Government Operations Committee concerning the security of confidential and top secret materials. Despite the challenges he faced while in office, Blattenberger had saved the government $13 million dollars by the time he resigned in 1961.[15]

The 1960s proved to be a time of growth and modernization. For instance, in 1967, the GPO installed a Linotron system, a high-speed electronic phototypesetting device that created a film negative for offset plate-making. Throughout the 1960s, Blattenberger's successor, James L. Harrison, modernized and reorganized the GPO. He even tried to move the GPO to a larger, more modern building. The longer it took to locate a suitable and available site, however, the more opposition to the plan mounted. In March 1970, Harrison announced his retirement and told the Joint Committee on Printing that he was "not envious" of the man who would follow him.[16]

The 1970s were a trying time for the GPO as the organization fell victim to the larger labor issues of the country. Before the new Public Printer, Nick Spence, could be sworn in, he had to go to a workers' rally to attempt to get some of his employees to leave the rally and return to work. Spence then asked the employees to give him a chance to conduct a complete review of GPO's wage structure.[17] Luckily, the workers did give Spence a chance. They returned to their jobs and Spence did as he promised, working to better the workers' situation. As the 1980s and 1990s ushered in the Information Age, the GPO continued to work to incorporate and use technology to its advantage. Computer and Internet technologies have changed the printing industry in far-reaching ways, creating new solutions and problems for both the GPO and the FDLP.

The Federal Depository Library Program: A Little More History

The origins of the FDLP date back to December 27, 1813, with a Congressional resolution calling for a single copy of all Senate and House documents to be sent to each college, university, and the historical society of each state.[18] On December 1, 1814, the Antiquarian Society of Worchester, Massachusetts, received the first shipment of government documents.[19] Though small, the importance of this first act cannot be underestimated as Ridley R. Kessler explains in his article, "A Brief History of the Federal Depository Program: A Personal Perspective:"

> Thus 34 years after the founding of the United States and in the middle of a war Congress took time to establish the rudiments of a national policy, based on the then original idea of sending free government publications to libraries. ... Congress created one of the longest running and most important partnerships in U.S. history—that of government and libraries.[20]

The FDLP's history began even before the GPO itself.

The FDLP remained unchanged until new legislation in the 1850s began to lay the framework for the modern FDLP. The Printing Act of

1852, for instance, provided for a Superintendent of Public Printing, which would later become the Public Printer, within the Department of the Interior, moving responsibility from the State Department. The act also provided for the election of public printers for the House and Senate and created the Joint Committee on Printing (JCP) to ensure that all printing was efficient and accurate. Then, in 1857, responsibility for both depository distribution and designating depository libraries was placed under the Secretary of the Interior, and the types of libraries that could be depositories were expanded.[21] By 1858, however, each state representative and territorial delegate could also designate depository libraries from the areas they served. U.S. senators soon followed in 1859, gaining the authority to designate one depository library in their states.[22] The post of Superintendent of Public Documents was created by an 1869 appropriation act; in 1895, the title was shortened to Superintendent of Documents.

A major leap was taken in 1895 when Congress codified all the laws surrounding government printing into a single comprehensive act. The Printing Act of 1895 was landmark legislation designed to eliminate waste and streamline distribution. The major parts of the Act included transferring document distribution from the Department of the Interior to the GPO, adding indexing duties to the GPO and Superintendent of Documents, and guaranteeing that government information was available to the public free of any charges.[23] Once organized under the 1895 Act, the depository system began to grow from the 420 depository libraries already established. The Printing Act of 1895 was the antecedent to Title 44 of the United States Code (44 USC 1901), which charged the Superintendent of Documents with "acquiring, classifying, cataloging, distributing to libraries and ensuring the preservation of Federal Government information products."[24] Title 44 also required all government agencies to submit all publications to the Superintendent of Documents for distribution to depository libraries. Within Title 44, Chapter 19 deals specifically with depository libraries, including their function and rules of operation.

Prior to 1922, each depository library received all government publications. So, even as early as 1922, libraries began to complain of waste, lack of space and staff, and unused collections—complaints that are still heard today. To answer these concerns, the GPO developed the "Classified List of United States Publications." Each library received two copies: one to keep and one on which to mark the selections they wished to receive and then return to the GPO.[25] This allowed libraries to be "selective" depositories, choosing only to receive some items rather than a copy of everything the government printed.

Over time, the FDLP continued to grow and evolve. In 1945, there were 555 depository libraries. Output had grown so much that the GPO was mailing an average of eight individual documents per library per day. After World War II, the GPO began to consolidate shipments into one box per library per day. The first Biennial Survey was also conducted after World War II in 1947 (more on this survey in Chapter 6).[26] The next big step for the FDLP, however, would come in 1962 in the form of the Depository Library Act.

The Depository Library Act of 1962 had a major impact on the FDLP but did not alter the basic doctrines of the previous laws. The 1962 Act increased both the number of depository libraries and the types of publications distributed. Importantly, this act also created regional depository libraries. Each state was allowed to have two regional depositories designated by its U.S. senators. Regional depositories permanently retain at least one copy of each publication made available regardless of format. They also are responsible for providing interlibrary loan, reference, and leadership to the selective depositories.[27] The structure of the FDLP was set in 1962 and has remained pretty much the same ever since.

Conclusion

Dating back to 1813 and 1860 respectively, both the Federal Depository Library Program and the Government Printing Office have taken strides to provide the American public with free, unrestricted access to federal government information. As a government documents librarian, you become a part of this history; as the Internet and Information Age promise to drastically change the GPO, the FDLP, and libraries, you may have a chance to make history.

From the Trenches

- Read enough to get a broad picture of the GPO and FDLP.

- Learn how your library earned depository status and why.

Endnotes

1. Daniel R. MacGilvray, "A Short History of the GPO." Available online at www.access.gpo.gov/su_docs/fdlp/history/macgilvray.html.
2. Joe Morehead, *Introduction to United States Government Information Sources*, Sixth Edition. (Englewood, CO: Libraries Unlimited, 1999), 16; MacGilvray, "A Short History."
3. MacGilvray, "A Short History."
4. MacGilvray, "A Short History."
5. "GPO's Living History: Adelaide R. Hasse." Available online at www.access.gpo.gov/su_docs/fdlp/history/hasse.html.
6. Robert E. Kling, Jr., *The Government Printing Office* (NY: Praeger, 1970), 27, 36.
7. MacGilvray, "A Short History."
8. Kling, *Government Printing Office*, 30–31.
9. Kling, *Government Printing Office*, 35.
10. MacGilvray, "A Short History."
11. MacGilvray, "A Short History."
12. MacGilvray, "A Short History."
13. MacGilvray, "A Short History."
14. Kling, *Government Printing Office*, 44.
15. MacGilvray, "A Short History."
16. MacGilvray, "A Short History."
17. MacGilvray, "A Short History."
18. Kling, *Government Printing Office*, 111.
19. Luke A. Griffin and Aric G. Ahrens, "Easy Access, Early Exit?: The Internet and the FDLP," *DttP: Documents to the People* 32 (3), 38.
20. Ridley R. Kessler, Jr., "A Brief History of the Federal Depository Library Program: A Personal Perspective," *Journal of Government Information* 23 (4), 369–370.
21. Kessler, "A Brief History," 370.

22. Sheila M. McGarr, "Snapshots of the Federal Depository Library Program," *Administrative Notes* 15 (11). Available online at www.access.gpo.gov/su_ docs/fdlp/history/snapshot.html.

23. Kling, *Government Printing Office*, 111–112; Kessler, "A Brief History," 370–371; McGarr, "Snapshots."

24. "Keeping America Informed: Federal Depository Library Program," U.S. Government Printing Office. Available online at www.access.gpo.gov/ su_docs/fdlp/pr/keepam.html.

25. McGarr, "Snapshots."

26. McGarr, "Snapshots."

27. Kling, *Government Printing Office*, 127; Kessler, "A Brief History," 371.

CHAPTER 3

The Modern GPO and FDLP: The Neo-Depository Era

In 2000, at the Fall Depository Library Council and Federal Depository Conference, a moderated panel entitled "Government Information Reference Services: New Roles and Models for the Post-Depository Era" coined a new term: "Post-Depository." The panelists were discussing how librarians needed to re-evaluate services in the electronic environment since users no longer needed to physically visit a library building to obtain information.[1] But this is wrong: They were not talking about a Post-Depository Era, but about a Neo-Depository Era. The prefix "post" means "after," but the time for depository libraries has not passed; however, the time *has* come for a new and different kind of depository.

Dating back to 1813 and 1860 respectively, both the GPO and the FDLP have striven to provide the American public with free, unrestricted access to government information. The shift to a predominantly electronic and online environment, however, has meant that the GPO, the FDLP, and all libraries must adapt and evolve to keep pace with both technology and user expectations. With change, however, comes conflict and uncertainty. The GPO is trying desperately to become a modern publisher, but the fact is that government agencies simply do not need the GPO to print and publish their works anymore. If the GPO is to live and thrive, it must reinvent itself, something it is certainly trying to do.

Librarians, too, must cope with today's changing technology, often playing a difficult balancing act between meeting user expectations of online fulltext access, while at the same time being a guardian and protector of information. The passion that librarians feel about all kinds of sources, from scrolls to digital collections, stems from a firm belief that all mediums are useful and important, and preserving information in all formats for all users is a worthwhile endeavor. Librarians are also struggling to find their place in the digital world. Perhaps this discord is best shown by two articles published back to back in the *Journal of Academic Librarianship* in 2005. The problem with these two articles is that they are both right. Both present totally divergent views and both have valid and articulate arguments. Published in May 2005, James A. Jacobs, James R. Jacobs, and Sinjoung Yeo's article, "Government Information in the Digital Age: The Once and Future Federal Depository Library Program," argues for a strong and robust FDLP that uses its traditional role in the new electronic environment. Then, in July 2005, John Shuler published "The Political and Economic Future of Federal Depository Libraries," a response to the Jacobs, Jacobs, and Yeo article. Shuler scolds librarians for their need to collect "stuff" and argues that libraries are for "access and mediation, not [physical] collections."[2]

The one thing that rings clear in both articles is that it is up to *all* librarians, whether in a depository library or not, to carve out their place in the world of digital government information. Both articles serve as a call to action for librarians. Taken together, they adeptly show the strengths and weaknesses of libraries and librarians. The challenge then becomes to find a middle ground where we can move forward and embrace new concepts of what libraries are and librarians do, while also being faithful to the traditional roles we've always had. Looking at where the GPO is today and where it is headed, librarians everywhere can easily get government information to the people who need it, whether they are part of a depository library or not.

The GPO and FDLP Today

The core mission of the GPO has remained the same over time: to keep America informed by producing, procuring, and disseminating government documents. The methods and means by which the GPO accomplishes these tasks, however, have changed drastically and will continue to change and evolve. The Information Age and the proliferation of electronic resources means that, to achieve its goal, the GPO must now capture, organize, maintain, authenticate, distribute, and provide permanent public access to digital information. Today, the actual printing is outsourced to private printers, allowing the GPO to concentrate on value-added services like Web-based information services, development of digital standards, preservation of digital publications, and authentication of digital information.

The modern GPO employs over 2,500 people and its main plant is a 1.5 million square-foot complex just five blocks from the Capitol building. Unlike most federal agencies, the GPO works more like a business in that it is paid for the printing it does and has a sales program where anyone can purchase publications. In fact, the *9-11 Commission Report* became a best seller at a price of only $10 dollars (which covered the printing costs), even though it was available online for free. The GPO also receives two appropriations each year. One appropriation pays for the Congressional printing needs and the other funds the cost of cataloging, indexing, providing online access, and distributing documents through the FDLP.

Any type of library, including those at land grant colleges, accredited law schools, a state's highest appellate court, and state libraries, can be a depository library, but it must either be chosen by members of Congress or by special provisions in the law according to Title 44. Each Congressional district generally has at least one depository library. Senators and representatives can also designate two libraries for their Congressional districts. Although these officials can designate libraries as depositories, they cannot de-select these libraries. Only the Superintendent of Documents can revoke a library's depository status (more on this later).

A library can also apply to be a depository library by submitting a justification for the request to its state library. The letter of justification should "address the library's eligibility for depository status, the library's unique qualifications for status, and the library's commitment to the goals of the Federal Depository Library Program."[3] The FDLP has a list of minimum requirements in the three areas of public services, staffing, and physical facilities that all depository libraries must meet to retain their depository status.

The FDLP includes approximately 1,250 depository libraries, both selective and regional, which are charged with ensuring that the public has free and open access to the government publications entrusted into their care. Under Title 44 of the *United States Code*, Chapter 19, Sections 1901–1916, the Federal Depository Libraries (FDLs) receive government publications free of charge in exchange for providing access to the collection. It is important to keep in mind, however, that the publications remain the property of the federal government. The FDLs are only custodians of the materials, not the owners, and they must pay for the personnel and the supplies for the upkeep of the documents collection.

Approximately 50 percent of the FDLs are academic libraries, making up the vast majority. At 20 percent, public libraries make up the second largest grouping of FDLs, followed by academic law libraries at 11 percent. Community colleges, federal agency libraries, state libraries, state court libraries, special libraries, federal court libraries, and military service academy libraries all fall at below 5 percent.[4]

Created in 1972, the Depository Library Council (DLC) assists the Public Printer, the Superintendent of Documents, and the GPO's staff in managing and operating the FDLP. The DLC consists of 15 librarians and serves as an advisory board only. Of the 15 members, at least half must work in depository libraries and have experience as a depository librarian. Each member serves a term of three years with five members retiring each year.[5]

Going Digital

In recent years, the GPO and the FDLP have begun a transition toward a more electronic collection. During the last two decades, technological developments and the Internet have resulted in a number of changes for both. Documents are no longer "produced, disseminated, controlled, and preserved" in the same way they once were.[6] In 1988, the first CD-ROM arrived in depository libraries and it continued to be the most prevalent electronic format through the mid-1990s. Public Printer of the GPO Bruce James declared that the GPO needed to "leap over the twentieth century into the twenty-first century" if it hoped to keep up with the rapidly changing environment.[7] The advent of the Internet has caused the GPO and FDLP to rethink its practice, since the Internet allows any government agency to publish its own material without going through the GPO. This also means that agencies can alter or remove documents without any notice.

The GPO's first entry into the world of electronic publishing and preservation came in 1993. The Government Printing Office Electronic Information Access Act (Public Law 103-40) became the basis for *GPO Access*, launched in 1994. *GPO Access* is "virtually the only Government website that provides one-stop, no-fee access to information from all three branches of the Government."[8] One of the main aims of *GPO Access* is to ensure that the public is able to find and obtain the various documents. With documents scattered about various agency and department Web sites, it is much harder for people to locate and obtain the information, especially since agencies can remove electronic documents at will. So, the GPO has taken on the responsibility of providing permanent access to electronic documents by copying them on to the *GPO Access* servers.

More than 10 years old, *GPO Access* provides users with a portal to a wealth of online government information from all three branches of government. *GPO Access* has won numerous awards and remains an example of the kind of outstanding project that the GPO, and the depository libraries, can create and manage in a digital environment. *GPO Access* links to more than 200,000 titles on the GPO server as well as other government sites. Though patrons were initially charged to access the site, by 1995, access was free to all users. Estimates show that users download more than 30 million files per month from *GPO Access*.[9] Since its debut in 1994, *GPO Access* has provided users with more than 1 billion documents. According to a 2003 study conducted by the Association of Research Libraries, 80 percent of depository libraries believed that access to electronic government information improved public use of government information.[10]

Rapid technological developments in digital publishing ushered in a number of challenges for the GPO and FDLP. The ease with which documents can be published, changed, and removed from agency Web sites is a particular challenge for long-term storage efforts. Therefore, many of these publications are never sent to FDLP libraries and are never included in the nation's bibliographic record system, resulting in a number of "fugitive" digital documents. As author Daniel P. O'Mahony argues, "the dynamic nature of electronic information and the ease with which data can be made to look 'official' raises concerns over whether the information the public has access to is genuine, authoritative, and untampered."[11]

Electronic access also affects the GPO and FDLP in a host of other ways. For instance, as authors Luke Griffin and Aric G. Ahrens explain, membership in the FDLP has lost appeal "since most of the important material is now available online."[12] They go on to say that "the Internet can be an obvious alternative to physical collections" since it allows information to be delivered directly to users.[13] Despite some feelings that all information is on the Internet, there are still some important publications that are only disseminated in print format. In many cases, electronic collections are only supplements of print collections. According to the FDLP Fact Sheet, "print provides a level of authenticity, permanence, portability, as well as a familiarity and ease of use that have yet to be matched by electronics." However, electronic formats do make it possible to disseminate information to more libraries. Further, by 2001, more than 60 percent of new titles released by the GPO were distributed as online documents.[14]

In 1996, the GPO conducted a "Study to Identify Measures Necessary for a Successful Transition to a More Electronic Federal Depository Library Program" through which it was determined that a predominantly electronic FDLP would be reached in five to seven years. However, just two years later, the GPO issued a manual for "Managing the FDLP Electronic Collection: A Policy and Planning Document." To meet the need to provide public access to online government documents, the GPO has brought "agency-disseminated Internet resources under the purview of GPO and [has] incorporate[ed] them into a digital archive."[15] In order to do this, the GPO obtains a copy of all agency documents or acquires the metadata for the documents so that a copy can be archived for preservation and maintenance. Though the documents remain under the control of the originating agency, they are linked through the GPO. To archive the documents, the GPO creates persistent uniform resource locators (PURLs) for each document. PURLs allow users to be redirected to the archived document even if the publication has been removed from the originating agency Web site.

As early as 1998, librarians were advocating for the GPO's need to "develop reliable systems to capture and preserve electronic government information for continuous and permanent public access."[16] O'Mahony successfully points out in his article "The Federal Depository Library Program in Transition: A Perspective at the Turn of a Century," that "files come and go, URLs and Web addresses frequently change, and there is a preference toward retaining only the most current information."[17] He also raises awareness of the issue of "lost" documents due to obsolete technologies. Librarians like O'Mahony called for a systematic approach to locating, obtaining, distributing, and preserving electronic government information.

The Internet and the move to a more electronic environment have prodded the GPO and FDLP to revise its policy on printing and disseminating government information. In the late 1990s, seven library associations joined forces to establish the Inter-Association Working

Group on Government Information Policy (IAWG) to push for legislation that would "strengthen the role of the Superintendent of
Documents and the Federal Depository Library Program" and "preserve and provide permanent public access to [government] information" while at the same time ensuring the authenticity of the
information.[18]

Essentially, the GPO no longer disseminates most government
publications in print format, relying on the Internet and agency
Web sites instead. Only a few documents, about 40 titles, are issued
in both print and electronic format. According to authors Gil
Baldwin and George Barnum, a "rigorous evaluation" takes place
before selecting a format for a publication.[19] Today, the FDLP
Electronic Collection is striving to be a complete digital library of
government information. The FDLP is currently in the process of
transitioning its collection of print, maps, and microform to an
online digital collection. In 2003, the Depository Library Council
recommended that the GPO create an online United States Library
of Public Information. The Depository Library Council agreed that
"in today's increasingly electronic environment, the need for a
United States Public Library of Public Information providing permanent public access, full cataloging records, widely accessible and
comprehensive in scope, becomes more of a national need. GPO's
pursuit of this library will address the current and future needs of
the new depository environment."[20]

The GPO is currently working with universities and other government agencies to collect and digitize historical documents that are
only available at a select few depository libraries. According to author
Miriam A. Drake, this project will convert more than 2 million printed
documents into a digital format.[21] Items in this digital "legacy collection" will include issues of the *Federal Register, U.S. Code,
Congressional Record, Monthly Catalog of United States Government
Publications, Congressional Bills, Public and Private Laws*, and
Statutes at Large. The initial retroactive digitization will incorporate
documents back to 1990 and will continue in 10-year increments.
GPO is also working with government agencies to develop consistent
standards for documents. Drake explains that the GPO hopes to
establish a Collection of Last Resort (CLR) that will house print and
microform copies of publications in addition to digital formats. The
CLR report, available via *GPO Access*, outlines the scope of the project. Drake goes on to point out that the GPO estimates it will take

between three and five years to locate all physical documents and to digitize the more than 2 million titles that will be included in the electronic collection accessible via *GPO Access.*

In the fall of 1999, the GPO established a Permanent Public Access (PPA) Working Group to discuss issues about preservation and access to electronic government information. According to the group's Web site, it is intended to identify a set of core values for access, develop practices for digital archiving, and identify "at risk" electronic information. It is difficult to tell to what extent this group has actively participated in developing policies and procedures for electronic government information. The Web site indicates that the last meeting took place in May 2001.[22]

Into the 21st Century

In December 2004, the GPO released its "Strategic Vision for the 21st Century." In this document, the GPO estimated that 50 percent of all government publications are now "born digital," meaning that they are published in electronic form first. Goals of this strategic vision include a "single authoritative resource to authenticate digital Federal documents," maintaining a digital repository for the documents, and "the flexibility to expand beyond text to include other future formats such as full motion video and sound."[23] The Strategic Vision report goes on to say that, to fulfill its goals, the GPO's Office of Innovation and New Technology will develop a Digital Content System, scheduled to be operational by December 2007, to catalog and authenticate government documents. According to the Strategic Vision, "it is clear that all future Government information, including text, graphics, still and moving images, and sound, will either be born digital or transformed into digital structure for manipulation, storage, and delivery to end users," though official journals such as the *Congressional Record* and *Federal Register* will continue to remain in print.[24]

In the report's conclusion, the GPO stated that "the times have changed and the GPO must change with them if it is to continue carrying out its core mission."[25] The GPO is currently working to create the Future Digital System (FDsys), the outgrowth of the call for a Digital Content System. The FDsys will enable federal government agencies or departments to create and submit content to the GPO that will then be preserved. All documents that are part of the FDLP will be included in the FDsys so that users can search, view, download, and print the information.[26]

In September 2005, the Depository Library Council issued "The Federal Government Information Environment for the 21st Century: Towards a Vision Statement and Plan of Action for Federal Depository Libraries, Discussion Paper." This report reiterated the emphasis on electronic resources and the need to develop new strategies and methods for coping with the digital age. The report states that all librarians "now have an opportunity to shape a vision of the government information environment of the 21st century with themselves as contributing participants."[27] The report also outlines four key areas where depository libraries can make the biggest impact: developing new roles for themselves in the nonexclusive government information environment, managing collections and delivering content, deploying expertise, and adding value.

One of the best statements in the Vision Paper regarding new roles for FDLs states that the current electronic environment "... could be interpreted to suggest that the Web had so diluted the exclusive role of the FDLs that the curtain call for the FDLP is at hand. However, a deeper scan of the status of FDLs in the current Web-dominated information environment reveals that there are several critical functions that FDLs should continue to fill in both the near and long terms and several new initiatives they should implement and maintain over time."[28] The Vision Paper then suggests three possible futures for the FDLP. First, it could "fold," deciding that everything is on the Web and the program requirements are too burdensome.[29] Second, the program could stay as it is and hold the status quo. Finally, the Vision Paper offers a third option where the FDLs and the whole library community work "in collaboration with the GPO, federal agencies, and other Web-based stakeholders to service the virtual FDLP collection on the Web."[30]

Conclusion

Clearly the GPO and the FDLP are willing to work with all libraries to develop a new FDLP that retains all the good stuff while evolving to cope with a new electronic environment and all the changes that come with it. For instance, we are a Google nation. Users love Google. Instead of fighting Google, why don't we join them? Librarians can easily see the weaknesses in Google, so why don't we lobby to make it better? The Vision Paper suggests making Google a more effective way to search for government information by having UncleSam include ALA/GODORT resources, certain FDL Web pages, Browse Topics from Oklahoma State University, and other government information resources without the .gov, .mil, and .us domains.[31] With the collective expertise of government document librarians, what else could we come up with to make things better for ourselves and users?

From the Trenches

- Don't get so tied up in the past or the future that you can't see the present.

- Change is hard, take time to relax.

- Work with partners and talk to other librarians.

- Be creative!

Endnotes

1. Proceedings of the Ninth Annual Federal Depository Conference. Available online at www.access.gpo.gov/su_docs/fdlp/pubs/proceedings/00proa. html.
2. John Shuler, "The Political and Economic Future of Federal Depository Libraries," *Journal of Academic Librarianship* 31 (5), 381.
3. Library Programs Service, Superintendent of Documents, *Designation Handbook for Federal Depository Libraries* (Washington, D.C.: U.S. Government Printing Office, 2003), 14.
4. U.S. Government Printing Office, *Keeping America Informed: Federal Depository Library Program*, A Program of the Superintendent of Documents. Available online at www.access.gpo.gov/su_docs/fdlp/pr/keepam.html.
5. "Depository Library Council: About." Available online at www.access.gpo. gov/su_docs/fdlp/council/aboutdlc.html.
6. James A. Jacobs, James R. Jacobs, and Sinjoung Yeo, "Government Information in the Digital Age: The Once and Future Federal Depository Library Program," *Journal of Academic Librarianship* 32 (3), 198.

7. Luke A. Griffin and Aric G. Ahrens, "Easy Access, Early Exit?: The Internet and the FDLP," *DttP: Documents to the People* 32 (3), 38–41.

8. Federal Depository Library Program, "FDLP Fact Sheet," 2, Available online at www.access.gpo.gov/su_docs/fdlp/libpro.html.

9. FDLP, "FDLP Fact Sheet," 1.

10. Miriam A. Drake, "The Federal Depository Library Program: Safety Net for Access," *SEARCHER: The Magazine for Database Professionals* 13 (1), 2.

11. Daniel P. O'Mahony, "The Federal Depository Library Program in Transition: A Perspective at the Turn of a Century," *Government Information Quarterly* 15 (1), 4.

12. Griffin and Ahrens, "Easy Access, Early Exit," 40.

13. Griffin and Ahrens, "Easy Access, Early Exit," 41.

14. FDLP, "FDLP Fact Sheet," 1.

15. U.S. Government Printing Office, "About *GPO Access.*" Available online at www.gpoaccess.gov/about.

16. O'Mahony, "The Federal Depository Library Program in Transition," 4.

17. O'Mahony, "The Federal Depository Library Program in Transition," 5.

18. Prue Adler, "The Times They Are a Changin' For Our Depository Libraries," *Journal of Academic Librarianship*, 388.

19. Gil Baldwin and George Barnum, "Government Documents for the Ages," *American Libraries* 32 (11), 38.

20. Drake, "The Federal Depository Library Program," 2–3.

21. Drake, "The Federal Depository Library Program," 3.

22. U.S. Government Printing Office. "Permanent Public Access Working Group to U.S. Government Information." Available online at www.gpo.gov/ ppa/index.html.

23. U.S. Government Printing Office, A Strategic Vision for the 21st Century (2004), 2. Available online at www.gpo.gov/congressional/pdfs/04strategic plan.pdf.

24. GPO, "A Strategic Vision," 5.

25. GPO, "A Strategic Vision," 10.

26. U.S. Government Printing Office, "Future Digital System (FDsys)." Available online at www.gpo.gov/projects/fdsys.htm.

27. GPO, "A Strategic Vision," 1.

28. Depository Library Council, "The Federal Government Information Environment of the 21st Century: Towards a Vision Statement and Plan of Action for Depository Libraries, Discussion Paper" 3. Available online at www.access.gpo.gov/su_docs/fdlp/pubs/dlc_vision_09_02_2005.pdf.

29. Depository Library Council, "Towards a Vision Statement and Plan of Action," 4.

30. Depository Library Council, "Towards a Vision Statement and Plan of Action," 4.
31. Since the writing of this book, Google's UncleSam has changed to Google U.S. Government Search and does include selected government sites with .com and .edu domains (www.google.com/help/about_usgovernment search.html).

CHAPTER 4

FDLP Requirements: Dragons and Beasts

Perhaps the loudest and most often heard criticism from librarians of all types, especially those in administration, is that the FDLP and GPO's requirements and standards for maintaining depository status are too burdensome, expensive, and stringent, especially since libraries can obtain much of the same information online for free without being a depository library. Unfortunately, in the last several years these criticisms, along with the evolution to the electronic environment, have caused the FDLP to experience a "downward trend" in library membership for the first time in history.[1] In 2004, librarians Luke Griffin and Aric Ahrens conducted a survey of 54 of the 56 libraries that left the program during the 2000–2002 fiscal years. The researchers found that the two most cited reasons libraries provided for leaving the FDLP were "staff or funding issues" (59 percent), followed closely by "availability of the same resources on the Internet" (43 percent).[2] Other reasons for leaving the program included "proximity to another depository" (23 percent), "space concerns" (19 percent), "diminished usage of the collection" (16 percent), "diminished value of depository status" (8 percent), and "inability to meet GPO standards" (8 percent).[3] Griffin and Ahrens go on to explain that many directors do not want to meet GPO budgeting and staffing standards for materials that their libraries can now access online.[4]

This disconnect between library administrators and depository librarians, the FDLP, and the GPO has often led to depository librarians ending up with the unenviable task of defending their library's depository status. Luckily for depository librarians, the GPO and FDLP took notice and began to really examine and address why libraries were leaving the program.

In 2002, the Depository Library Council created the Subcommittee on Attrition and Retention (SOAR). This subcommittee of the Operations Committee is charged with developing "different techniques to encourage and support depositories to remain active in the Federal Depository Library Program" in addition to investigating and analyzing a host of different ideas.[5] The cumulative effect of the new electronic environment and the GPO and FDLP's response to the loss of library membership has ushered in a new paradigm. As a result of this shift, the advantages of being a depository library have been enhanced and the requirements for being a depository aren't nearly as burdensome as they were in the past.

Slaying Dragons: Criticisms and Requirements

It seems that librarians will always have to struggle with the "it's-all-online" syndrome of users. What is sad, though, is when we as librarians do that to one other. In a 1999 article entitled "New Technologies and Old-Fashioned Economics: Creating a Brave New World for U.S. Government Information Distribution and Use," Diane Smith, former Chief of Reference and Instructional Services at Pennsylvania State University, asked, "Should not librarians be experimenting with new and different ways to provide users with assistance in locating government information in a timely and economic manner rather than attempting to shore-up the concept of an FDLP network that has outlived its relevance in today's world?"[6] In my opinion, we must not throw the baby out with the bath water. There are many good reasons for building and strengthening the FDLP network.

One of the best resources for defending depository status is located on SOAR's "Stay with the Program" Web site, which provides access to a collection of materials gathered and published by SOAR, including presentations by depository librarians, cost/benefit savings studies, and incentive documents. SOAR's materials provide depository librarians with effective and concrete information for responding to criticisms, including "staff or funding issues" and "availability of the same resources on the Internet"—the two top reasons for leaving the program as cited by Griffin and Ahrens in their study.

For instance, SOAR resources hammer home that "it" isn't all on the Internet. Most information dating from pre-1996 is not digitized, and some materials (for instance, maps) aren't always appropriate for the electronic medium, especially if they are large and detailed. In 2000, 53 percent of new titles were published electronically.[7] In addition, just because it is online doesn't mean it is free to everyone. The model is that if you are a depository library you get the materials at no cost, so even if the government produces an online resource, it may not be free for all libraries. *STAT-USA, USA Trade,* and *Environmental Health Perspectives* are examples of databases that depository libraries get free access to through the FDLP while non-depository libraries have to pay for access. Public Printer Bruce James reiterated this point in the plenary session on Strategic Vision at the 2005 Spring Depository Library Council Meeting. When asked if depository libraries would continue to have free access to digital collections, James replied, "That's the deal ... you give your time and service and currently your real estate, and we give you this information for free. Every time we talk about how we are going to handle the future, we always say that anything we do must go to the Depository Libraries without cost ... That's our commitment to you."[8]

Moreover, the GPO, the FDLP, and depository librarians are addressing many of the staff and funding issues as well as the complaints about the regulations being too stringent. According to the Vision Paper, the "GPO is gradually reducing the amount of oversight of depositories and the paperwork required of them. While GPO gives guidance to remaining depositories, it has begun to devote fewer resources to their inspection and oversight."[9] The depository environment is evolving in new and exciting ways, providing FDLs the opportunity to participate in the program in new and dynamic ways as well.

The Manual(s)

Even the manual for depository libraries is being revamped. In 2005, the GPO and FDLP decided to create a new manual for depository libraries. This new manual will combine the *Federal Depository Manual* (originally published in 1983 and revised in its entirety in 1993 with later portions revised as needed) and the *Instructions to Depository Libraries,* which was revised in 2000, into a single online document called the *Electronic Federal Depository Library Manual* or "E-Manual." In addition to consolidating these two documents, the new E-Manual also addresses the changing nature of the program, updates content, and provides examples of best practices and lessons learned. The E-Manual is organized into these 15 chapters:

1. Library Services Content Management (LS & CM) Organization

2. Legal Requirements, Minimum Standards, and Policies

3. Federal Depository Status

4. Public Services

5. Depository Collections

6. Bibliographic Control

7. Maps

8. Preservation

9. Housing

10. Staffing

11. Partnerships

12. Regional Services

13. Primarily Electronic Depository Collections

14. Disaster Preparedness and Recovery

15. Federal Libraries

Appendix A: Core Collection

Appendix B: Acronyms, Glossary

Appendix C: For Library Directors

Appendix D: Selective Housing Agreement

First introduced at the 2005 Spring Depository Library Council Meeting, seven of the 15 chapters had been posted for the documents community to review as of August 2006. Three chapters in the new E-Manual—"Maps," "Primarily Electronic Depository Collections," and "Disaster Preparedness and Recovery"—are entirely new. This E-Manual is a significant update of the previous material and signals a shift in the relationship between the GPO, FDLP, and depository libraries. For instance, as previously discussed, the GPO is no longer the only place where libraries can obtain government information. So, in order to maintain participation by libraries, the GPO and FDLP have adopted a gentler and friendlier tone and attitude. Instead of a seemingly draconic list of rules and regulations, the new E-Manual is a much more helpful document. While the older manuals took a punitive "you must do this or we'll revoke your status" tone, the new E-Manual's approach is much more along the lines of "here are the things you have to do and here is how we can help."

To compile the E-Manual, the GPO and FDLP called for volunteers to create a team for each chapter, a practice they used to create both the previous manuals. Made up of people from the GPO, the FDLP, and librarians, each team consisted of a team leader, team researchers and writers, a new depository librarian, a subject consultant, and a reviewer.

Each chapter of the new manual begins with a section on what is new and important, with changes highlighted. The next section covers what is legally required under Title 44, followed by coverage of what is mandatory according to GPO policy. With these requirements explained, the chapter teams were next given an opportunity to be creative; The E-Manual diverges from earlier manuals with sections on "Tips, Practical Advice, and Lessons Learned," "Did you realize you don't have to...", and "Important for Library Administrators." These three new sections allowed the teams to provide real life examples and advice as well as to address common misconceptions, creating a much more dynamic and useful manual.

Virtual Depository

Another interesting and exciting outgrowth of the electronic environment is the opportunity for a library to become a Virtual Depository Library (VDL). This option allows depository libraries to concentrate on building and managing virtual collections rather than physical ones. The advantages of transitioning to or becoming a VDL are that your collection is available to the public 24/7, and less staff time is spent on the processing, circulating, shelving, and storage of tangible items.

Libraries can choose to be either a "Full Virtual Depository" or a "Partial Virtual Depository." Full Virtual Depositories must select all electronic items and up to 20 core titles in tangible format. They also must provide full cataloging of all their depository selections and a higher level of technology, such as scanning equipment and chat reference. A Partial Virtual Depository can select electronic and print resources, but should concentrate on developing and building a strong electronic collection. Partial Virtuals do not have to provide full cataloging or the same level of technology as Full Virtuals.[10]

Not surprisingly, both types of virtual depositories are required to have Internet access and a well maintained government documents Web page. Also, the minimum technical requirements for computers are very important for virtual depositories. The FDLP publishes recommended specifications and minimum technical requirements for depository workstations on the FDLP Desktop. While the minimum technical requirements have been criticized as too expensive and burdensome in the past, most of the requirements now come standard on new personal computers (PCs). Also, keep in mind that *all* the library's computers aren't required to meet the specifications. The number of depository workstations depends on the size and scope of the depository. Basically, libraries require a sufficient number of computers meeting the minimum standards to efficiently and effectively serve patrons. The technical requirements just aren't that stringent anymore. More on Internet access and Web pages in Chapter 7, "Public Services Issues."

Virtual depositories are a new model for depository libraries and are still being defined and molded. The first official virtual depository is at the University of Arizona (U of A). Together with the U of A School of Information Resources and Library Science and the GPO's Library Programs Service, the main library decided to initiate a pilot program in 2002 to assess the implications of migrating to an electronic environment on both the users and the library. The project was extensive and well documented, providing the library community with a huge amount of data. Overall, their project was a huge success. The U of A library found it did indeed save space, staff time, and money. It also found that users preferred to access government information online.[11] While this project involved a large research library at a Carnegie Research Level I university, its results and success definitely show that becoming a virtual depository, even for major research libraries, is a real and effective possibility. Similar projects in other types of depository libraries are needed but the potential is limitless.

Relinquishing Status

Depository membership is not for every library, but for those that have already obtained depository status, any plan to relinquish it should be given careful consideration. Everything is a trade off, and the goals and missions of some depository libraries may not fit with the new virtual environment; however, leaving the program is a long and tedious process, and once depository status is relinquished, you may find it harder to rejoin the program than it was to become a depository library in the first place.

If your library is considering giving up its depository status, it involves much more than just saying you aren't going to participate anymore. Remember that all the material you receive through the program does not belong to the library. The library is merely the custodian of the materials. If you leave the program, it is very likely that all the materials the library has received will have to be returned. This means you will have to generate a list of all the materials the library has received and offer them to the regional and other depository libraries so they can take what they need. The library will then have to ship the materials to their new homes and clean up the catalog and any Online Computer Library Center (OCLC) holdings to reflect that the library no longer holds them. Then, of course, since some of the materials will be crucial items for the library's collections, replacements will have to be purchased. Once the regional and all the other depository libraries have picked over the holdings, the library can request to keep materials, but it is only a request. The regional depository librarian has the final say as to whether a library can retain materials once it leaves the program.

In a 1999 article, "Closing Down a Government Documents Collection: The Experiences of Millsaps College," Edward Kownslar does an excellent job of explaining the process Millsaps College went through to relinquish its depository status. The process began in November 1996 and was completed in January 1999, a total of two years and three months.[12] The first thing Millsaps was required to do was pull all the documents from the stacks, including those that had been cataloged and classified with Library of Congress Subject Headings, which had to be reclassified with SuDoc call numbers. The offers list was 1,500 pages long, not including the microfiche collection. For the microfiche, the regional librarian allowed Millsaps to create "lists that included general ranges of SuDoc numbers."[13]

Kownslar does not indicate if he agreed with the decision or what, if any, impact relinquishing depository status had on the library's users, but his article does convey the amount of time, effort, and expense it takes to dismantle a depository collection.

When my library was considering relinquishing status in 1999, many of the same arguments were voiced: Maintaining a government documents collection was too expensive, most of the resources were free on the Internet, running a collection eats too much time and uses too much staff, as well as all the other standard complaints. Two things made the difference. The first was money. The library had already recently spent money on trying to improve the collection. When we loaded just one book cart with a sample of the materials that we would have to return, it made an impact. The administration had not realized that the materials would need to be returned and replaced. That replacement cost as well as the resources and staff time to dismantle the collection meant spending a great deal of money to lose materials. The second thing that made a difference was that a librarian was willing to step up and take on the collection. I don't think most librarians realize that they can negotiate job duties in many cases. My supervisor rearranged my schedule to provide me more time to work with the documents collection. People were so glad someone was willing to take on the documents collection, they were happy to help make up any slack in other areas. If the opportunity arises to be a documents librarian, grab it!

Conclusion

In my opinion, the FDLP is not dying; it is growing and evolving. While it may be experiencing growing pains, the potential is there for the FDLP and depository libraries to be more visible and more effective than ever in getting government information to people. Abandoning the program and starting from scratch is a silly notion, especially when the FDLP provides us with such a strong foundation of knowledge and experience. If nothing else, identifying ourselves as depository libraries and librarians gives us a unique identity and a collective voice, which helps us ensure that government information remains accessible to all.

From the Trenches

* One person can make a difference. Step up.

* If your library is considering relinquishing status, do some research and make sure you and your library are fully aware of the consequences.

* If you do relinquish status, you must notify the Superintendent of Documents in writing and by fax.

* Consider all options and be creative.

Endnotes

1. Luke A. Griffin and Aric G. Ahrens, "Easy Access, Early Exit?: The Internet and the FDLP," *DttP: Documents to the People* 32 (3), 38–41.
2. Griffin and Ahrens, "Easy Access, Early Exit," 40.
3. Griffin and Ahrens, "Easy Access, Early Exit," 40.
4. Griffin and Ahrens, "Easy Access, Early Exit," 40.
5. *Administrative Notes: Newsletter of the Federal Depository Library Program* 23, no. 08 (June 15, 2002). Available online at www.access.gpo. gov/su_docs/fdlp/pubs/adnotes/ad061502.html.
6. Diane Smith, "New Technologies and Old-Fashioned Economics: Creating a Brave New World for U.S. Government Information Distribution and Use," *Journal of Government Information* 26 (1), 24.
7. Federal Depository Library Program, "FDLP Fact Sheet." Available online at www.access.gpo.gov/su_docs/fdlp/libpro.html.
8. U.S. Government Printing Office, *Plenary Session on Strategic Vision* (Washington, D.C.: U.S. Government Printing Office, 2005), 13.
9. Depository Library Council, "The Federal Government Information Environment of the 21st Century: Towards a Vision Statement and Plan of Action for Federal Depository Libraries, Discussion Paper," 4. Available online at www.access.gpo.gov/su_docs/fdlp/pubs/dlc_vision_09_02_2005.pdf.
10. E-Manual Chapter 13 Draft, 2–3. (Unpublished author's draft copy).
11. Atifa Rawan and Cheryl Knott Malone, "A Virtual Depository: Arizona Project," Proceedings of the 12th Annual Depository Library Conference (2003). Available online at www.access.gpo.gov/su_docs/fdlp/pubs/proceedings/03pro_rawan.ppt.

12. Edward Kownslar, "Closing Down a Government Documents Collection: The Experiences of Millsaps College," *DttP: Documents to the People* 27 (4), 11.
13. Kownslar, "Closing Down," 11.

CHAPTER 5

Networking and Training: You Are Not Alone

Of the 44 fully accredited library schools in the U.S., all but three offer a course with the word "government" in the title. I suspect that if I had taken the "Government Information Sources" class while I was at the University of Tennessee it would have been helpful, but I did not plan on being a government documents librarian. However, if you are still in school and interested in government documents, by all means take the course if your school offers one. While the courses are all different, at the very least you will get a good introduction to the kinds of government resources available, even if your professor does not go into much detail about the GPO or FDLP. Some of these classes can be very broad, covering state and local documents as well as UN documents.

If you are like me and did not take the course while in school, do not worry. On-the-job training is a good way to learn too. In fact, Yang's survey found that almost 63 percent claimed self-instruction, or on-the-job training, as the primary method of learning about documents. Following self-instruction, in-service training was a very distant second with 17 percent claiming it as their primary method for learning.[1]

One of the strangest feelings I had when I became a depository coordinator was one of isolation. I suddenly had responsibility for an entire collection that had its own rules and classification scheme. Luckily for me, I had a great regional librarian and fantastic colleagues throughout the state who helped me figure out what to do and how to do it. I quickly learned that other people in the documents community were my greatest resource.

The Regional Depository

One of your most influential advocates should be your state's regional depository librarian. Each state has one, but some states share the responsibility between two libraries. In Alabama, for instance, the University of Alabama in Tuscaloosa and Auburn University in Montgomery work together to provide regional depository service to the state. In Colorado, the regional depository status is shared between the University of Colorado at Boulder and the Denver Public Library. Regional depository libraries must meet all the obligations of a selective depository in addition to meeting several other obligations.

Ideally, the regional librarian serves as a coordinator, mentor, and leader for all the selective depositories in the state. The lines of communication between regional librarians and their state's selective depositories should be wide open. One of the regional librarian's most important duties is to facilitate networking and training among his or her selective depositories. If you are a new depository librarian and your regional librarian has not contacted you, then you should contact him or her. Invite your regional librarian to come visit your library for a tour of the collection. It is also important for you to keep your regional librarian informed about any problems or issues that arise in your library. Your regional librarian should be available to talk to your library staff and administration to address any concerns or problems they may have with the regulations and goals of the FDLP.

Regional depository librarians are also responsible for coordinating their region's collection as a whole to ensure that the collection is comprehensive and complete. This means that the regional library houses a copy of every government document produced, except those that are superseded or otherwise authorized for discard by the Superintendent of Documents. This is also why you must follow your regional librarian's procedure for discarding documents. After five years, selective depositories can ask to remove items from their collection, but the decision to allow a library to discard materials is entirely up to the regional librarian. To make this decision, regional librarians will look to see if anything on your discard list matches what they need or want; if it does, they will add the items to their collection. If they do not need it, they will offer your discards to other selective depositories in their region. This process allows libraries to replace damaged or lost items. However, the regional librarian may decide that you need to retain items based on your user population.

Peers

Your fellow depository librarians are your greatest asset and resource. No one knows what it means to be a depository librarian like other depository librarians. There are many ways to get in contact with other librarians in the documents community, so seek out a mentor to help you or ask your regional librarian to recommend someone. The documents community is one of the friendliest and most active of all library groups. Do not be afraid to ask for help or advice. Go visit other depository libraries in your state and do not limit yourself to one type of library. Just because you work in an academic library does not mean that the public depository library or a law library does not have anything to offer you. All documents librarians are in this together, and we should all be prepared to support each other no matter what our local situation is. We are documents librarians first.

GODORT, MAGERT, and More

GODORT is the American Library Association's Government Documents Round Table. ALA can establish a round table when there are at least 100 ALA members who are interested in a particular area of librarianship that is not covered in one of the 11 ALA Divisions. Formed in 1972, GODORT is an active and resource-rich organization that covers all aspects of government documents librarianship. GODORT, like the other ALA round tables, provides an important vehicle for discussion, promotion and marketing, and education.[2]

Maps, however, are special and have their own map and geography round table: MAGERT, a round table that deals with all kinds of cartographic information, not just government maps. MAGERT is a fantastic resource for government documents librarians, since most government documents collections include maps of some variety and managing them can be a challenge. Though they are difficult to catalog, circulate, and house, maps can also be real gems within your larger government documents collection. If you find yourself with a map collection within your documents collection, MAGERT, the world's largest map library organization, is the place to turn for help.[3] To join GODORT and MAGERT, you have to be a member of ALA first, but once you are a member of ALA, you can join as many round tables as you like if you are willing to pay the dues. Round table dues range from $3 to $20 for regular members while students can often join for less; both GODORT and MAGERT are $20 each for regular members.

Two other organizations can also be helpful, depending on the scope of your collection. If you have a strong law collection then the American Association of Law Libraries (AALL) can be a helpful organization. AALL is a national organization with a large membership, covering all aspects of law librarianship. A second national organization that may prove helpful to government documents librarians is the Special Library Association (SLA).

If your home state or geographic area has a documents organization, join and be active in it. I was really lucky because Georgia has a fantastic group of documents librarians. They generally meet twice a year after the fall and spring depository conferences, and also have their own listserv. Most state library associations also have an interest group or round table devoted to government information. If there is not a group in your state, try a neighboring state. The Southeastern Library Association, for instance, has a government documents round table. Keep in mind that you can always work toward creating your own group.

The key is to join the groups that you believe will be the most useful to your particular situation. Membership is expensive and being an active member in all of them would be impossible. Being a truly active member makes the difference though; otherwise you are just paying dues. Pick the two or even three that best fit your needs and participate in those. For me, I joined ALA/GODORT and my state's organization. But just because I was not a member of the other organizations did not mean I could not call on them for help.

GPO/FDLP Conferences

There are three main conferences offered by the GPO and FDLP: the Interagency Depository Seminar, the annual Fall Federal Library Conference, and the annual Spring Federal Library Council Meeting. If you can attend these conferences, you will definitely benefit from both the content of the programs and the opportunity to meet and mingle with other documents people. Even though the conferences are free to attend, the reality of most budgets, either institutional or personal, means that the travel costs are still too expensive for most people to attend all three. So, you may have to choose which of these three conferences you want to attend. There is a lot to consider when choosing an event to attend, especially if you are investing your own money in the experience.

If you are a brand-spanking new documents librarian, you should do everything you can to attend the Interagency Seminar, which is packed with training opportunities. The training is presented by the federal agencies that produce the information products and services. For instance, you would get to learn all about the census materials and services from the people who actually produce them at the Census Bureau. Attendees also get to go on behind-the-scenes tours of some of the federal agencies, such as the Library of Congress, the Senate Library, and the Patent and Trademark Office. The Interagency Seminar is an excellent opportunity to get an overview of government documents and to see some things and places you would not be able to see as a regular tourist. The seminar is usually in late July and lasts an entire week. Registration is limited to about 60 people and preference is given to first time attendees and new documents librarians.

With all that said, you do not have to attend the Interagency Seminar to benefit from the spring and fall annual conferences. Both conferences include meetings with GPO and FDLP officials, presentations by documents librarians, various updates, and open sessions. The fall conference is always in Washington, D.C., and tends to be somewhat larger than the spring conference, which is always somewhere west of the Mississippi River. Both conferences are really high-quality and well worth attending.

Listservs

Listservs are also a fantastic way to keep connected to the government documents community, and there more than 30 different lists that documents librarians can join. The two primary ones are GPO-FDLP-L and Govdoc-L. Begun in 2002, GPO-FDLP-L is the official way that the GPO communicates with depository libraries, and each depository library should have at least one person subscribed to this list. Anyone can sign up for the list, and GPO-FDLP-L also has a searchable archive page.

Govdoc-L is a moderated discussion forum co-hosted by Pennsylvania State University and Duke University. The list is open to anyone who would like to subscribe and is not affiliated with any government, government agency, or professional organization. For documents librarians, Govdoc-L is truly a lifeline to a wealth of knowledge and help. One of the main ways people use Govdoc-L is for asking reference questions. You can also get help with administrative and management questions and share ideas for promotion and outreach. There always seems to be someone online who can help, but the list also has a searchable archive just in case. Be warned, though: Govdoc-L is an extremely high traffic listserv.

Depending on your interests or areas of responsibility, there are also more specialized lists available. These lists vary in numbers of subscribers and amount of traffic. For instance, GPO-BUSPUBS-L for GPO business publications has more than 7,000 subscribers while the list for agricultural publications, GPO-AGRIPUBS-L, has about 50. The neat thing about lists is that you can sign up for free, and if you find the list is unhelpful, you can leave with just a few mouse clicks. With all these options though, it is easy to get overwhelmed. One method for managing the huge amount of e-mail these lists generate is to learn how to use the filtering function in your e-mail client. Most e-mail programs have a way for you to send certain messages to a specific folder, bypassing your inbox so you can read them later. If you cannot get your filter set up, ask someone on Govdoc-L for help.

RSS Feeds and Blogs

In addition to listservs, there are also RSS feeds and blogs. RSS stands for "Really Simple Syndication" or "Rich Site Summary." To subscribe to an RSS feed, you usually have to download a news reader that translates the code into short messages, like headlines. If you are interested, you click on the link and read the fulltext. Most readers are free and easy to download and install. The GPO has two different RSS feeds available, "FDLP Desktop News and Updates" and "*GPO Access*: What's New." Once you download the reader, all you have to do is subscribe to the RSS feed as you would a listserv. In addition to these

GPO RSS feeds, there are several other federal government RSS feeds including:

- FirstGov U.S. Government RSS

- Library Census Bureau News on the Site

- Computer Emergency Readiness Team RSS Channels

- Department of Defense News Reader Feeds

- Department of Education RSS Feeds

- Equal Employment Opportunity Commission (EEOC) RSS News Feed

- U. S. Geological Survey (USGS) Earthquake RSS Feeds

- National Aeronautics and Space Administration (NASA) RSS Feeds

- National Institutes of Health (NIH) News and Events

- National Weather Service Experimental Listings of Watches, Warnings, and Advisories by State and Territory

- National Weather Service: National Hurricane Center/Tropical Prediction Center RSS Feeds

The GPO's RSS Main Page keeps an updated list of RSS feeds (see the address in the resources section), and, like listservs, you will most likely want to pick and choose which RSS feeds to subscribe to depending on your interests and needs.

Some individual depository libraries have started their own RSS feeds. For instance, Georgia State University's library in Atlanta has created a number of different RSS feeds for its users, including one for government information and maps. RSS feeds are an excellent way for libraries to get information out to their users. You will most likely have to work with your systems people to get one started, but once you do you will have a powerful tool.

Blogs are another way of using Internet technologies creatively within the government documents community. For instance, the Depository Library Council created a blog to use as an open forum for librarians to discuss their papers "Toward a Vision of the Government Information Environment of the 21st Century: A Draft Outline" and "The Federal Government Information Environment of the 21st

Century: Towards a Vision Statement and Plan of Action for Federal Depository Libraries, Discussion Paper." A second blog, Future Digital System (FDsys) Blog, published by the GPO, is directed toward discussing the functionality of the FDsys.

GPO's "Ask A Question" and Knowledgebase

The GPO has created a knowledgebase of the questions and answers compiled from the "Ask a Question" Web form. The knowledgebase is searchable across the entire database or you can limit your search to one of three categories: the online bookstore, *GPO Access*, or FDLs. Once you choose a category you can then limit your search even further by selecting a subcategory. The database and Web form are easy to use. If neither the knowledgebase nor asking your question through the Web form works, you can still call direct Monday through Friday, 7 A.M. to 9 P.M. EST at 888-293-6498.

The Literature

Professional literature is yet another way to keep abreast of current themes and issues in documents librarianship. While a general search on "library literature" will retrieve all sorts of interesting results, there are three specific journals for government documents librarians. The first is *DttP: Documents to the People*, the official publication of GODORT. *DttP* is published quarterly and includes a variety of different articles, as well as GODORT news and business. If you are an ALA/GODORT member, a subscription is included in your dues. Even if you are not a member, you can still subscribe to the journal. Most round tables and library organizations at least have a newsletter that will often have notices about training, workshops, and meetings.

The *Journal of Government Information* and *Government Information Quarterly* were combined into one journal, *Government Information Quarterly*, which was first published in 2005 by Elsevier. The publisher decided that given the scope and readership of the two journals, it made sense to combine them into a single publication. An interdisciplinary journal, *Government Information Quarterly*, includes scholarly refereed articles on such topics as policy, information management, technology, e-government, and other issues relating to all levels of government all over the world.

Books

There are not very many books dedicated specifically to government documents, but there are a few good ones that can help. One of the newest books is *United States Government Information* by Peter Hernon, Harold C. Relyea, Robert E. Dugan, and Joan F. Cheverie, published in 2002. The book you will hear the most about, however, is Joe Morehead's *Introduction to United States Government Information Sources*. Now in its sixth edition, Morehead's book is a standard text. The strength of this book is its coverage of both print and nonprint specialized and general resources. No documents librarian should be without a copy. Another good guide to navigating government resources is Judith Schiek Robinson's *Tapping the Government Grapevine: The User-Friendly Guide to U.S. Government Information Sources,* now in its third edition. *Tapping the Government Grapevine* is an excellent resource for learning how to do government documents reference. While the Morehead and Hernon books do devote a little time to the structure and history of the GPO and FDLP, all three works concentrate on locating and using government information rather than managing a government documents collection.

The only work dedicated to managing a government documents collection is *Management of Government Information Resources in Libraries,* edited by Diane H. Smith and published in 1993. A collection of different essays on a variety of topics, this book offers a broad look at administrative issues relevant to managing a government documents collection. Although the work is older, it still contains some good advice and information.

Conclusion

There are many ways to stay connected to the government documents community and there is no right or wrong way to network. But as you explore all these options, keep in mind what did and did not work for you. Networking is not a one-way path. The more you learn and the more experience you gain, the more you will need to share with the documents librarians who follow you. So, if you had a really great mentor, offer your services to a new librarian. If you like to publish, then write articles about topics that interest you. Do not limit yourself, however, to just the two journals mentioned above. There are many library journals, both scholarly and otherwise, so publish in those as well. Also, GODORT and your local documents organizations are fantastic ways to be active and meet people. Offer to present or host events. Find your niche and give back to the documents community.

From the Trenches

- The duties of the regional depository librarian are covered in Chapter 12, "Regional Services," of the new E-Manual.

- Communicate with your regional librarian.

- Participate in regional and national events and workshops.

- Make sure to follow your regional librarian's guidelines for discarding documents.

Endnotes

1. Zheng Ye (Lan) Yang, "An Assessment of Education and Training Needs for Government Documents Librarians in the United States," *Journal of Government Information* 28, 429.
2. Government Documents Round Table, American Library Association, "Bylaws." Available online at www.ala.org/ala/godort/godortbylaws/bylaws.htm.
3. Map and Geography Round Table, American Library Association, "About MAGERT." Available online at magert.whoi.edu/about.html.

CHAPTER 6

Managing and Administering: The Big Picture

As a depository librarian, managing and administering the collection is one of your most important tasks, as you will be responsible for the oversight of the entire collection. This means you will have to manage up, down, and across the food chain. Chances are you will have at least one staff person who reports to you and countless others you will depend on to get the job done. You will need the cooperation of your peers in your own department who are already busy with their own jobs and duties. Communicating and working with peers and middle management in other departments is crucial, as is working with both your library administration and the GPO and FDLP. This area, more than any other, allows you to let your diplomatic and organizational skills shine. There are also FDLP requirements the library will have to meet in terms of staffing, housing the collection, and disaster recovery. There is a lot to learn and master about being an administrator and manager, and the great thing about learning in a documents setting is you have the opportunity to learn within the big picture of the library as a whole.

When Things Go Right with People

In many ways, working with other people is the most challenging and most rewarding part of being a manager and administrator. In the new E-Manual, there is no set formula for determining the amount of staff needed to effectively manage the depository. The old formula called for one hour of staff time for each 1 percent of items selected.[1] Basically, the requirements call for as many people, professional and paraprofessional, as you need to get the job done right. Staffing also depends on the size and scope of the library and individual circumstances. There must be a depository coordinator, but this person can have other duties too, as in my case. The depository coordinator is responsible for the coordination of the program (this person is not responsible for doing all the tasks required by the FDLP, but for ensuring that they get done), documenting the library's efforts, and serving as the communication conduit between the library administration and the regional depository and the GPO. Being a depository library is a library-wide commitment, and as depository coordinator you'll need to tap into other staff for specialized help.

The trick then becomes getting other people to do more work, not a particularly easy thing to do. Differing philosophies can get in the way, as can personalities and unwillingness to adapt to new work flows. One of the things I was most proud of when I was a documents librarian in Georgia was the buy-in I generated from other departments. One of the best lessons I learned was that enthusiasm is really contagious. Preparing for that reinspection was hard, but any time I went to talk to another department or person, I put on my happy face. If I believed that the collection could be saved, they believed it too. The more excited I got, the more excited other folks got.

I also learned the power of communication. I sent out library-wide e-mails each week so that folks could be involved with the progress being made. These e-mails served to educate folks as well as create a sense of involvement. They didn't have to be long or complicated and I always ended with a note to contact me with any questions or concerns. I was careful to thank people for their help, too. By involving everyone and referring to the collection as "ours," I began to get people invested in the collection's success.

If I needed a department or an individual to take on a task or do something they'd already been doing differently, I always tried to approach it from their point of view. I'd meet with them, explain what I needed done, and then ask them what they thought and if they could help. Nothing shuts people down faster than an authoritative approach and being told they are doing something wrong. We worked through the issues together. I also tried to make things as easy as possible for people, whether that meant creating "cheat sheets" for certain procedures or changing how I did things. Because I showed concern for them and willingness to adapt my routines to make their jobs easier, folks were very willing to do whatever they could to help me. I had an incredibly supportive immediate supervisor, too. All I had to do was tell her what I needed and she managed to get it for me, whether it was equipment or time away from other duties to prepare for the reinspection. I was very lucky and worked with a very special staff.

When Things Go Wrong with People

Some folks just won't cooperate no matter what you do, and sometimes there is nothing you can do to make someone work with you. Perhaps you have rubbed them the wrong way, or maybe they are just unhappy and determined to spread that unhappiness. There are also people that thrive on controversy and turmoil. Encounters with these folks can be at best frustrating and at worst hurtful. The best strategy is to continue to be professional, flatly refuse to participate in any games, and protect yourself and the collection.

Ideally, your supervisor will be someone who you can turn to for help. However, if your supervisor is no help or, worse, is the problem, then keeping a written record can help you. Ask for things in writing and keep copies of e-mails. If the person consistently ignores you and doesn't reply, keep a record of the e-mails you sent asking for a reply. Track your efforts! Then if there is a problem with either a GPO requirement or your evaluations, you have the necessary documentation to prove that you have tried to get things accomplished. If you cannot get the help of your supervisor or the director, turn to your regional. Don't suffer alone: Ask for help.

Knowledge is another resource you can rely on to help you. Few statements get the attention of administrators like "We are required by law to …". The GPO and FDLP enabling legislation is Title 44 of the U.S. Code, which deals with public printing and documents. Now, I'm not suggesting you read the law cover to cover, but there are some parts of it that can definitely help you. For instance, Chapter 19 of Title 44 (44 USC 19) deals specifically with the Depository Library Program. Chapter 19 Section 1909 covers the requirements and conditions of depository libraries. Section 1911 is where you'll find the clause about free public use: "Depository libraries shall make Government publications available for the free use of the general public. …"[2] The rules and duties of regional depositories are found in section 1912. While reading legal text can be tedious, knowing that the laws are there and where to find them can help you gain an understanding of depository rules and write justifications for needed materials and policies. This applies to the new E-Manual as well. Make sure your supervisor and your director have copies of both Title 44 and the E-Manual. Place copies at the reference desk too.

Do your very best to avoid entering into an adversarial or accusatorial relationship with people. While it may be hard sometimes, remain professional and courteous. Don't make it personal, even if the other person does. Just continue to advocate for the documents collection.

Paperwork

Paperwork is a big part of any administrator's job and the depository coordinator is no different. The GPO and FDLP are required by law to check up on depository libraries, and while the Inspection Program is being phased out, they will still need to monitor depository libraries. One way they do this is through the Biennial Survey (see Appendix B). Conducted every two years, the Biennial Survey (44 USC §1909) is a self-report conducted by depository libraries that allows the GPO and FDLP to gather information on the status of the libraries.

The survey is submitted online, but you can download a copy of it and fill it out before you sit down to submit the information. The survey isn't hard to complete, but allow yourself enough time to get the necessary information from other departments and the people in your library. The 2005 survey was 17 pages long and asked questions that ranged from policy decisions on binding tangible items to the willingness of libraries to maintain government documents on local servers for others to access.[3]

Another report is the Self-Study; however, this report is part of the Inspection Process, and whether or not depository libraries will still be required to complete this report is uncertain. The Self-Study was designed to help depository coordinators assess their library's compliance with Title 44 and other GPO regulations. Each year, GPO's Library Program Services would request Self-Studies from a group of libraries determined from their last inspection date. The Self-Study would then be used to determine if an onsite inspection was needed.[4] Chances are a new form of the Self-Study will be used as a self-reporting tool for depository libraries.

Aside from reporting tools, paperwork also appears in the form of lists. The GPO will send you a list of shipping lists; when you receive one, check off the list number from the list of shipping lists. The shipping list then serves as a packing list for materials that the library is supposed to receive. Are you following me? It isn't that hard really. You get two lists. One is a list of the packing lists and one is the packing list itself. You must use these lists to verify that you have received everything you were supposed to receive. The general rule is that you keep these lists for three years. Sometimes, however, there are separate lists for special formats. For instance, libraries receive a separate list for USGS maps sent directly to the depository libraries from the USGS. While all these lists may seem a little neurotic, they do help you keep track of what you have and have not received. Once you see them and work with them, it's easy to keep track. There are also tools for helping with list management. For instance, depository libraries can download lists from the Federal Bulletin Board and the Shipping Lister. If you find you didn't get something you were supposed to receive, there is Web form to claim the item.

Another paperwork responsibility is to develop the policies the depository collection needs and keep them updated. According to the GPO, you need seven policies in place: an Access Policy, a Collection Development Policy, a Binding Policy, a Documents Replacement Policy, FDLP Internet Use Policy, Public Services Guidelines for Government Information in Electronic Formats, and a State Plan (the State Plan is under the purview of the regional librarian). This may seem like a lot, but some of the policies are quite short and there are all kinds of examples on the Internet. Use examples from both the GODORT Handout Exchange and other depository libraries like yours as a template to ensure that the depository policies and the library's policies mesh. Also, it is a good idea to make these policies readily available. Post them on a Web page and create a notebook for the reference desk. Make sure everyone knows where the policies are and encourage them to ask if they have questions.

Other examples of paperwork include keeping statistics and creating annual reports within the library. Often, measuring what librarians do is difficult. Keeping statistics on the number of materials received and cataloged, reference questions answered, circulation, and the like can be a good measure of a librarian's activity and assessment. Keep track of what you tried to do even if it didn't work. Report efforts you made and what you learned from them. Just because something didn't work doesn't mean it wasn't worth a try.

Disaster Recovery

The E-Manual has an entirely new chapter covering disaster preparedness and planning and is full of suggestions and advice for being prepared. I will never forget asking for a copy of my library's disaster plan so I could make sure the documents collection was covered and being told the library didn't have one. Much of the material in this chapter is common sense, but planning for a disaster that may or may not come is usually low on the priority list. Generally, something devastating has to happen first before disaster plan development moves up as a priority, and then of course it is too late. As a documents coordinator, there are things you can do to be prepared even if your library as a whole is lagging behind.

One suggestion in the E-Manual is to maintain a list of your documents. If your library's online catalog server and the backups are housed in different locations, the data is pretty safe. If not, have the system administrator or technical services folks run you a report, then save it to a disk, and take it home. That way you have a record of your library's documents collection. Make copies of other essential documentation and take them home, too. If you are uncomfortable with taking materials home, send them to your regional or another depository librarian to house for you. Keeping copies of important documents off-site is always a good idea.

Another important consideration is that since the depository library is the custodian of the government documents and has the responsibility of replacing them, if a disaster *does* occur and documents are lost or damaged, make sure that the cost of replacing or repairing government documents is included in any insurance estimate. It is also a good idea to decide on a disaster recovery company ahead of time. Just remember that all you can do is all you can do. Being prepared for a disaster is primarily up to the library administration, and sometimes the best you can do as a depository coordinator is provide the necessary materials and information. If you have any doubts, send them an e-mail asking if the materials were received and to let you know if they have any questions. When you get an affirmative response, print that e-mail off and take it home.

You gave them the information; if they didn't bother to read it, it isn't your fault!

Housing the Collection

As depository coordinator, you are also responsible for the physical maintenance and housing of the collection. I found that the collection was much easier to maintain when kept together and organized with the SuDoc classification scheme. In the past, many libraries integrated government document materials into the Library of Congress collection in order to get them either in the card or online catalog so people could find them and the items could circulate (more on cataloging in Chapter 8, "Technical Services Issues"). As online catalogs improved, documents no longer needed to be integrated into the LC collection for either circulating or cataloging. Also, the documents that had been integrated into the main library collection were the most substantial and important pieces, so when the administration looked at the collection, all they saw were the items deemed unworthy of LC classification. This was important to me, because one of the arguments for relinquishing status was that all we received were pamphlets and maps. People had forgotten about all the monographs received through the FDLP that were integrated into the LC collection. As I began to pull items from the LC collection and reintegrate them into the government documents collection, some people expressed concern that patrons would have a hard time navigating the SuDoc classification. Keeping the government documents collection together and organized in SuDoc order didn't seem to bother the library patrons. I just made sure that the documents collection was clearly marked with signs directing people to the reference desk if they couldn't find what they were looking for in the stacks. What I found was that most library users didn't realize they were looking at two very different classification schemes; they were just looking at letters and numbers. The advantage was that the government documents collection was all together on the shelves so I could manage and promote it much more easily.

Maintenance also includes weeding and superseding the collection. After five years, depositories can weed items through the needs and offers service. If something doesn't fit your collection or isn't being used, weed it. Offer it to a library that can use it. Make sure you supersede items as they arrive. It was a wild day when I realized the collection I had just assumed responsibility for hadn't been weeded or superseded in about 10 years. A regular routine of weeding and superseding materials really helps on space issues.

The main thing to remember is that the care, maintenance, and preservation standards for the documents collection must be equal to that of the rest of the library collection. Another thing to watch out for is that if your library is an older building, housing for documents must meet the standards of the "Americans with Disabilities Act."

Contacting the FDLP or GPO

There are a number of ways to contact both the GPO and the FDLP. First, there is a searchable Knowledge Base that anyone can access, including a way to ask a question via e-mail if you do not find an answer within the Knowledge Base. You can also call the GPO from 7:00 A.M. to 9:00 P.M. toll free at 866-512-1800 Monday through Friday, except holidays. They also have a fax number, 202-512-2104, and a mailing address: U.S. Government Printing Office, Mail Stop: IDCC, 732 N. Capitol Street, NW, Washington, DC 20401.

Conclusion

While the managerial and administrative tasks can seem overwhelming, just remember to break things down into manageable pieces. It really isn't as hard as it seems. Use this opportunity to explore whether you would like to pursue a career in library management and administration.

From the Trenches

- Always say "please" and "thank you."
- Try to make the documents collection a library-wide project.
- Remember to weed and supersede.
- Use other libraries and GODORT to write your policies.
- Make sure the documents collection is included in your library's insurance policy.
- Make sure the housing and maintenance of the collection are equal to the rest of the library's collection.

Endnotes

1. Janet Fisher and Tim Bryne, "FDLP Myths and Monsters," Spring Federal Depository Library Conference and Depository Library Council Meeting, April 19, 2005. Available online at www.access.gpo.gov/su_docs/fdlp/pubs/proceedings/05spring/myths_monsters.ppt.
2. "Title 44—Public Printing and Documents Chapter 19—Depository Library Program," U.S. Code Online, Section 1911. Available online at www.access.gpo.gov/su_docs/dpos/title44.html.
3. U.S. Government Printing Office, "2005 Biennial Survey." Available online at www.access.gpo.gov/su_docs/fdlp/bisurvey/05bsq-final.pdf.
4. U.S. Government Printing Office, "Self-Study of a Federal Depository Library." Available online at www.access.gpo.gov/su_docs/fdlp/pubs/fdlm/self stud.html.

CHAPTER 7

Public Services Issues:
Making the Government
Documents Collection Sparkle

The focus of a documents librarian's public services strategy should be on access and visibility. The nice thing is there are many ways to accomplish these goals, and you can really pick and choose your activities according to your and your library's strengths. The public services activities are also some of the most fun parts of being a documents librarian and it's an area where you can really use your creativity. However, the goals of the FDLP are not always completely compatible with the library administration's goals or even the personal beliefs and values of your co-workers. Sometimes you have to use a good bit of tact and finesse to meet both the expectations of the FDLP and your own library administration.

But fear not! There are strategies and methods for working around these issues when you discover them. Most of the time, working with government documents within the public services sphere is one of the most rewarding and entertaining aspects of government documents librarianship. By breaking down the main activities and FDLP requirements, you will begin to see how your own creativity and enthusiasm can bring about success no matter what.

It's All About the Access, Silly!

One of the primary functions of a depository library is the "fundamental obligation to provide free public access to depository information resources and to minimize other barriers to public access to the library's depository facilities, collections, and services."[1] Make no mistake about this one; the FDLP is pretty serious about providing access to the collection, whether print or electronic, but the FDLP is also very tolerant. The key is to strive to provide *exactly* the same level, or higher, of service for the government documents collection as is provided for the rest of the library collections.

For example, if the library's monographs circulate for two weeks, then the government document monographs should also circulate for two weeks. If the library's journals do not circulate, then the government document journals are not required to circulate either. The FDLP's regulations and best practices are not complicated; in fact, they are really just common sense. Each type of media brings its own special circumstances to the table. So, when thinking about how to provide the best access to your documents collections, be sure and take all the different kinds of materials into consideration.

Tangible Stuff

Even though the number of tangible products issued by the GPO is dwindling, there are still plenty of tangible items produced today. The majority of depository libraries will have legacy collections to maintain and manage, so providing access to a tangible collection will remain an important aspect of any government documents librarian's duties. Even if you are managing a totally virtual depository collection, you may still have a need to refer patrons to libraries that do have tangible collections. Having a knowledge and feel for these tangible collections is always helpful.

While this may sound simple, providing access to a tangible collection is a multifaceted operation that can demand the utmost in creativity, because we are not just talking about books and journals. A tangible collection includes CD-ROMs, DVDs, maps, microfiche, and random objects like stickers, globes, patches, posters, and art. You must provide access to all of these things as well.

The things you can just take off the shelf or out of the drawer and look at are the most simple. Having these items stored on publicly accessible open stacks is ideal. If you have the collection in an open stack area where anyone can browse and use the collection, you are in great shape. But what if there is a problem getting to your open stacks? It seems that in almost every library I've ever visited the government documents collection is tucked away in a corner, usually in the basement or in one of the oldest parts of the building.

The collection I managed in Georgia, for instance, was located in a dark corner on the second floor of the library—not terrible, since I could get the burned-out lights replaced, but the library had no elevator. The collection was totally inaccessible to anyone with any sort of physical disability that prevented them from climbing a flight of stairs. My only option to try and overcome this issue was signage. I peppered the reference area and the information and circulation desks with signs telling patrons that if they needed help retrieving items from the second floor, they should ask for assistance at the reference desk. It wasn't perfect, but it was the best we could do within the limitations of the library's physical structure. Even if your library has elevators, they can malfunction. Having some ready-made signs to place in strategic areas is a nice and easy thing to do. It also shows that you are proactive and that access to the tangible part of your collection is important to you and your library. Be creative if you have physical access issues. Demonstrating that you are doing the best you can with what you have goes a long way with both the FDLP and your library users.

Microfiche can also prove to be a bit challenging, not because they are hard to house or use, but because the microfiche reader/printers are expensive to buy and maintain. Further, very few places even produce microfiche anymore. Electronic access has made the medium antiquated and obsolete. Many librarians find themselves waiting for their current reader/printer to die, fearing it will not be replaced and that even if a new one is placed on the budget, it will likely be a low priority, leaving the library with no way for patrons to use the microfiche. Having any resource with no way for people to use that resource is frowned upon by the FDLP and does not make much sense anyway. The worst thing you can do is let the collection just sit there.

If you have a problem with providing access to your microfiche collection, there are things you can do. First, check your item selections and de-select any of the materials you are still receiving in microfiche. You can also contact your regional (see Chapter 5, "Networking and Training") to see if it wants to take the collection. You can also offer the collection on the National Needs & Offers List (see Chapter 8, "Technical Services Issues"). Going through your regional, the microfiche collection will be offered to other depository libraries in your state and then offered to depository libraries across the country. If you cannot provide access at your library, then offering your collection to other depositories that can provide access is the very best thing you can do. In some cases, offering your collection will help replace collections lost either by fire or natural disaster. Another option would be to make a cooperative agreement with another library in your area. This will allow your library to check out the microfiche to patrons who can then use another library's reader/printer. This situation is certainly not ideal, but at least it allows your patrons to use the microfiche and retrieve the needed information. I have even known researchers who have their own microfiche readers at home! So, circulating the microfiche collection is not that far-fetched.

While microfiche is disappearing, content on CD-ROMs and DVDs is still being produced. Computers have added a whole new complex issue to the world of government documents librarianship: The need to work with information technology (IT) people. IT people are, by nature, concerned with network integrity and security, as they well should be. Librarians, however, tend to be concerned with providing the most information to the most people in the most efficient way, as librarians should be. When IT people and librarians meet, it has to be about compromise. I became extremely frustrated when the IT people at my institution refused to allow patrons to run government documents CD-ROMs on PCs connected to the Internet. They simply would not let anyone write or copy data to the hard drive of a PC that was connected to the Internet. No matter how much I pleaded and argued that the CD-ROMs contained live links to other government resources and that some would not run without installing software, they would not bend.

Making sure all the CD-ROMs and DVDs circulate is a very good way to provide access. That way, if your library has policies that limit the use of CD-ROMs and DVDs, patrons can at least take the materials home and use them there. You should continue to lobby for at least one computer to be designated as the government documents workstation. Designating a computer as a documents workstation does not mean it cannot be used for other things—it just means that documents use is the priority for that PC. In my case, we settled on a second reference desk computer. Since those PCs did not have the same security setup, people could use the CD-ROMs there. Neither the IT people nor I thought it was a perfect solution, but it gave us a starting place, and once you have a place to start from, you can move forward—or at least sideways!

DVDs posed similar problems to CD-ROMs. We did not even have a DVD player in the building when we received our first DVD from the

GPO. Most new PCs today come with at least the capability to view DVDs. The FDLP also issues yearly minimum workstation specifications. These guidelines are really nice, because they give you something from the FDLP to hand to your library administrator and IT people that states exactly what they expect at least one computer to have and do in your library. The important thing here is that I did all I could to ensure access. Few of my solutions were perfect, but by making the effort we satisfied the FDLP (and me) that we were doing all we could to provide the best access available. Circulating the GPO materials is one of the very best policies you can develop. If at all possible, circulate everything and lend everything via interlibrary loan as well. Since I was in a university library, the general public could not check things out, but they could go through the local public library and get whatever they needed. The FDLP wants to see the documents collection being used. Now, remember, the key is to make sure the government document collection's accessibility is equal to or greater than the library's other collections. Do everything you can to make the collection accessible within the policies of your library and you will be fine.

Virtual Stuff

Access to online materials is just as important to the FDLP as access to tangible items. The first thing a depository library must have is a written policy for electronic government resources that includes provisions for free access for all users; the FDLP has guidelines to help you write a policy if you do not have one. This means that if you are an FDLP library, you must allow anyone to use both the tangible collections and the computers to access the electronic collection, no matter if you are private school or law school library. The only exceptions are highest appellate court libraries. What you do not have to do is provide for free copying and printing or storage media. Your normal and customary charges apply. If your students, for instance, get charged 10 cents a page for copying and printing, then it is fine to charge depository users 10 cents a page. What you must do is offer the same service to depository users as you offer to your other users. So, you cannot deny depository users a printout if they are willing to pay the normal charge. By the same token, if you sell storage media like floppy disks, CD-ROMs, or other storage media to one group, you must sell them to depository users for the same price.

Another interesting aspect to managing electronic access is the use of Internet filters, which prevent people from using certain keywords to search or blocks certain URLs. If your library uses filters, you must ensure that those filters do not limit access to government resources. Depository libraries must allow depository users access to computers without a filter or ones where a librarian can disable the filter. One of the best examples of why this is so important is that filters can hinder users from accessing the vast amount of health-related information that the government provides. A depository user seeking information on breast, prostate, or cervical cancer may have a difficult time getting through a filter to a government resource. The use of filters in libraries is a highly charged issue, especially in public libraries, where they are most often used to protect children and young library patrons. Be careful not to get dragged into a heated debate over the issue of using filters in general. You need to stay focused on getting depository patrons nonfiltered access. Signage that informs patrons that your library uses filters is always helpful, as is letting users know they can ask the government documents librarian for assistance in finding information on certain topics, such as medical issues. Find out what kind of filtering software is being used and learn what it can and cannot do. If your library's filter blocks certain URLs, you may be able to instruct people how to get to a government resource like Medline Plus directly without having to type in filtered keywords. However, keep in mind that simply allowing access to Internet domain names ending in ".gov" is not enough to ensure access to all government information.

Depository library Web pages play multiple and important roles in any government documents collection, and the FDLP encourages all depository libraries to have at least a basic Web page. For the purposes of public services, a well-designed Web page should do two important things: It should tell users the purpose and goals of the collection, and it should identify the government documents librarian and provide contact information. A Web page can also provide direct links to a variety of government resources. Cataloging your depository selections for inclusion in your local holdings is the ultimate goal (more on bibliographic control in Chapter 8). Sometimes, however, it is easier and more efficient to create simple finding aids and lists of the resources that are most pertinent to your users and post them on your Web page if you can.

If you do not have a Web page, you should definitely try and get one started. The amount of freedom and latitude you will have to create your pages will vary depending on your library's policies, but you should definitely work toward developing at least a basic Web page. GODORT has created a template that libraries can use to get started with a basic Web page. The template, available for free, is designed so that it can be loaded and used immediately with very few alterations. The links included on the templates touch on all levels of government and are considered both key resources and stable Web sites. So, the links should not change, meaning the maintenance of the template is minimal. Very good instructions are also provided. And, again, be creative. If you have never created a Web page yourself and do not want to learn or have the time, partner with someone. Contact local schools and colleges and inquire about getting a student to do a practicum or project.

Reference Services

No depository library is required to maintain a separate service desk just for government documents. The key is to provide the same level of service for depository users as for any other users. For instance, if the library is open extended hours for exams, then depository users should be allowed to access the collection during those extended hours as well. Remember that consistency between collections and user access is the goal. So, for example, if your library provides chat reference to your primary user group, you must also provide that service to depository users. If you answer reference questions via e-mail or telephone for your primary user base, you must offer these same services to depository users. This means the rest of the reference staff will have to be trained by you to answer basic government document questions. You, however, will remain the point person and the tendency will be to send every documents question received to you. Usually, this is okay, except, for example, during tax season. No one wants to be summoned from his or her office every time someone wants a 1040EZ form.

The best way to train people is to do it without their even knowing they are learning something. Still using tax season as an example, highlighting the Internal Revenue Service (IRS) site on the Web page and then creating step-by-step instructions on how to find and download the different tax forms is an easy way for you to help your colleagues. E-mail the instructions to the reference staff and post a "cheat sheet" at the reference desk. Written instructions provide your colleagues with the information at the point of need. Remind people that users have to pay for printouts and copies and provide a phrase for the librarians to use when explaining that they cannot give tax advice. This relatively small investment in time and effort will have a big payoff: You have taught the other librarians something, made the information easier for them to use and find, and provided them with information needed to handle some difficult situations that may arise.

Holding in-house training is also a good option, although finding a time when everyone can meet may prove difficult. But providing training sessions, creating tip sheets, and communicating with the rest of the staff will make your life easier and help your library provide the best government documents reference it can. My best advice is to always praise and never criticize. It is always difficult when you need people to work for you but you do not supervise them. By making their participation in the government documents program as easy as possible, you will slowly win converts from all over the library. Never make colleagues feel bad or inadequate for referring questions directly to you. Always ask what you can do to make this more convenient for them.

Referrals are also an important part of the public services equation. Each selective depository collects and specializes in different kinds of resources. So when a user comes to you with a question you cannot answer or is looking for a resource you do not have access to, you should feel free to call on another depository librarian or refer the user to another depository library. For instance, patrons needing older materials may need to visit the regional depository library since it will typically have the largest and most complete collections. Questions involving legal resources are another good example of specialized government documents reference where you may want to contact a law librarian or send the user to a law library. I always knew I could call on my counterparts and my regional to help me get the users the information they needed (see Chapter 5 for more on networking).

Promotion

Library marketing and promotion is by far the most fun of all the FDLP requirements. Library marketing and promotion is about awareness and education, and there are tons of ways to connect users to resources whether your library has a promotions budget or not. While you should definitely extend your library's marketing efforts to all potential depository users, including the library staff, your primary user population, and the general public, you do not have to extend everything to everybody all at once. Break things down into measurable parts and market specific resources to specific user groups. One of the very best things about library marketing and promotion is that it can be whatever you want it to be.

An excellent way to get your feet wet with marketing is to piggyback on already established library, campus, or community events. If your library is creating a Fourth of July display, ask if you can include a few government documents. Setting up tables at appropriate campus and community events is another way to get involved without having the entire burden of the event on your shoulders. Community health resources are a really good example of a topic that fits nicely into health fairs. Also, if you have a digital camera, take some pictures and post them to your Web page. Make your displays and events virtual as well as physical.

To help encourage libraries to market their collections, the FDLP has created some wonderful resources with all kinds of ideas and suggestions. One of the simplest and best resources available is the variety of FDLP graphics you can download from the FDLP desktop. I would advise using these graphics everywhere you can. Use them on range finders, map cases, and every single handout and presentation you do. I even made little laminated tabs with the logo that stuck out of items used on displays. Make sure people know the resource comes from the government documents collection. In fact, since government publications are not subject to copyright regulations, you can use any government publication or image to highlight your collections.

The FDLP provides a variety of supporting materials that depository libraries can order, including bookmarks, classification charts, decals, posters, brochures, finding aids, and a host of other items free of charge. Depending on the federal budget, GPO staff members are available to visit your library and provide training on various resources like *GPO Access*. The FDLP has even created a screensaver for libraries to download. Pick and choose what best fits your library's needs and atmosphere and just start trying different things. The goal is to create interest, increase awareness and visibility, and educate users as well as other librarians.

Instruction

Library instruction is a fantastic way to incorporate all the facets of public service. Chances are the more awareness and visibility you create the more demand for instruction will grow. It may grow slowly, but it will grow. Generally, there are two kinds of instruction: in-person and online. According to Jeffrey M. Wilhite's article "Internet versus Live: Assessment of Government Documents Bibliographic Instruction," students learned as much from an online class as they did from in-person instruction. The in-person instruction, however, received more positive feedback than the online sessions.[2] Both methods are effective means of educating people, but personal contact with a librarian seems to make a difference in the users' overall satisfaction with the class.

Since both methods are effective, it makes sense to use both. In fact, creating an online tutorial is an excellent way to prepare for an in-person class. The benefit of the online version is that users can access it whenever they have a need. Keep in mind that the electronic world changes very fast and often without notice, so keep your online content basic and general while always including that all-important contact information. Also, there is no need to reinvent the wheel. There are some really wonderful tutorials and handouts on the Internet that you can link to and use for inspiration. One of the best resources is ALA's GODORT Handout Exchange, a huge collection of all kinds of finding aids and tools.

In-person instruction also offers a whole host of opportunities. Generally, when people think of library instruction, they think of classes coming to the library, but today, all librarians need to consider getting out of the building on occasion. Going to the users and offering to speak on their home court is an excellent way to generate enthusiasm and goodwill. For instance, offer to demonstrate *Ben's Guide to U.S. Government Documents for Kids* to local schools, or send out fliers and e-mails about *Ben's Guide* to education departments of local colleges and universities. The governmental medical resources also provide fantastic opportunities for library instruction. You can target local nursing programs and hospitals and offer to show them where the consumer health resources are and how to search PubMed.

Public speaking can be a scary prospect, so when you begin to advertise that you offer classes in government resources, start small.

Pick a topic or resource that really interests you and that you are already pretty comfortable using, and advertise it to smaller groups to see if you get any nibbles. If you get no response, do not feel like you have failed. It takes years to develop an active instruction program and a client base for your classes. Your very first public presentation might simply be a brief introductory announcement explaining that you offer classes on how to find government information. If you speak to the right audiences and provide handouts with contact information, you will start to get calls.

Team teaching is also a good way to build an instruction program. If your library already has classes scheduled, ask if the instructors would be willing to include links to government resources on their handouts. Make sure your colleagues, both inside and outside of the library, know that you are available to team teach with them. Partnering with people from your campus or community is a great way to get your instruction program noticed. Use your imagination and be creative in getting the word out about government document resources.

Signage

Proper signage is also an important part of public services for any library collection. Ideally, patrons should be able to easily navigate their way to and use the government documents collection just by following the signage. No matter what signage your library has or does not have, however, you must display the depository emblem in a prominent place. The FDLP prefers that the emblem be visible from outside the library. The FDLP suggests placing the emblems on your library's entrance doors.

Be creative with your collection signage and change the signs occasionally. (I usually changed them each semester.) Making general "Lost? Ask for Help at the Reference Desk!" signs is always a good idea. I've also made signs advertising the electronic version of a resource, using a clear plastic sign holder to display it on the shelf next to the print version. You can also highlight specific electronic resources at key times. For instance, drawing attention to the State Department's Travel Warning Web page during vacation months will catch the attention of travelers and provide a good service. Remember to use that FDLP logo!

Conclusion

There are many ways to make sure your documents collection is accessible and visible, but do not get overwhelmed. As T. Scott Plutchak, director of the Lister Hill Library of the Health Sciences at the University of Alabama at Birmingham, once said, "We can do anything, but we can't do everything." Concentrate on the things you must have, like providing access, and then pick and choose the marketing and promotional activities that make the most sense for your situation. You may not have the staffing to launch an instruction program or the budget to travel to other locations to teach. In that case, concentrate on creating awesome Web pages and signs instead.

From the Trenches

- The guidelines and rules for the public services aspects of the FDLP are covered in Chapter 4, "Public Services," of the new E-Manual.

- Depository libraries must provide free access to government resources to the general public.

- Make sure to have a written policy for the free use of electronic government resources for all users.

- Refer users to other libraries when needed and offer to have users referred to you.

- Market and promote the collection to all users.

- Access and services for the government documents collection should be comparable to or greater than the access and services for other library collections.

- Depository libraries must allow users the opportunity to use a computer without a filter or with the filter turned off.

- Depository libraries must display the FDLP emblem in a prominent location.

Endnotes

1. Janet Scheitle, "Depository Library 301: Electronic Depository Manual," Proceedings of the Annual Fall Depository Library Conference & Council Meeting, October 16–19, 2005, Slide 24. Available online at www.access. gpo.gov/su_docs/fdlp/pubs/proceedings/05fall/index.html/janet_ scheitle_manual_oct05.ppt.
2. Jeffrey M. Wilhite, "Internet Versus Live: Assessment of Government Documents Bibliographic Instruction," *Journal of Government Information* 30, 570–571.

CHAPTER 8

Technical Services Issues: The Devil Is In the Details

I always thought I was a closet technical services librarian, and when I became documents coordinator, I had the chance to find out if it was true. And guess what? It *was* true! I love the technical services stuff, and I used my position as documents coordinator to learn all I could about the technical services department's work flow, technology, processes, and all the rest. I know I was lucky. Not all technical services departments are open to having a public services person come in and poke around, but I worked really hard to create goodwill. For instance, I let them know I was really interested and wanted to learn. As a result, I even got to learn some cataloging. I'll tell you, the first time I cataloged a document and then looked it up in the Online Public Access Catalog (OPAC), it was quite a feeling. I had always wanted to catalog, and even just copy cataloging was really fun. I learned more from those folks than I ever could have imagined. If you can get yourself involved in technical services, do it. Even if you don't become a pseudo-member of the technical services department like I did, you are still going to have to work with it and do a number of technical services tasks yourself. Don't let this put you off—it is one of the best opportunities for professional growth and lifelong learning that documents librarianship offers you.

Collection Development

Collection development is one of those areas that often crosses departmental lines. For the purposes of documents, it more closely matches activities found in technical services departments, such as collection analysis and acquisitions. The goal is to develop the best collection possible, concentrating on the most appropriate content in the most appropriate formats for your user base. To do this you will need to look at the library's main collection. What kinds of commercial materials have been selected and for what areas? Take a look at your library's collection development policy; hopefully your library has one. Then, once you have a handle on what your library collects and why, you can make your item selections to complement the commercial collection.

What are item selections? When you choose documents to receive, you do not choose titles; instead you choose a group of titles within an item number. This means you will sometimes choose a group of materials that you will have to house for at least five years just to get one title you need. So, it is very important to choose wisely, especially for tangible items. For instance, if you work at a depository library at a university with a strong program in military history, selecting the item numbers that include materials from the U. S. Army and Navy history centers would be a very appropriate selection. So, for example, you select the item number 0344-G, "The U.S. Army Campaigns of World War II." That item number includes seven titles: *Army Lineage Series* in print, *Historical Analysis Series* in microfilm, the *Historical Study Series* in print, the *Army Historical Series* in print, the *U.S. Army in Action* Series in print, the *U.S. Army Campaigns of World War II* in print, and the *American Forces in Action Series* in print. That is a lot of print material. Selecting all the military history resources the GPO offers has the potential to take up a good bit of physical space. If you have space issues, you may want to ask the history department what they focus on in order to make more targeted selections.

Well, that's just dandy, but how do you know what item number to pick and what is included in those numbers? There are some creative tools to help you figure out what item numbers to select. One of the most helpful is the Documents Data Miner (DDM) hosted by Wichita State University. The DDM uses a structured query language (SQL) server to create a database with all kinds of searching options from the data downloaded from the FDLP's records. You can search by title, SuDoc stem, item number, agency, format, and status. There is also a search function where you can search for the selections of depository libraries. Not only can you get a list of what your library has selected, but you also can see what other libraries select. The DDM is a powerful and flexible collection development tool worth exploring.

Another tool to help with collection development is the Item Lister. The Item Lister works a lot like the DDM. Updated weekly, the Item Lister allows depository libraries to download their selections in a variety of different ways. For instance, you can get a list of just what you select, only the things you don't select, or a complete list with items marked with a 'Y' for selected and an 'N' for not selected. When the new Integrated Library System (ILS) for documents is completed, it will also be a great tool. The online catalog combines the Catalog of U.S. Government Publications and the New Electronic Titles list into one database. This catalog will include records from July 1976 forward and display all the depository library holdings. So, there are plenty of tools out there. Find the tool, or the combination of tools, that works best for your situation.

Your list of item selections is your library's profile. Each year you have to review your library's profile. You can drop item numbers any time using the Item Amendment Web form, but you can only add item numbers during the Annual Item Selection Cycle. The cycle usually lasts about a month and allows depository libraries to add and drop item numbers. During this cycle is when the GPO recommends doing a Zero-Based Review, meaning that depository coordinators look at each item number and evaluate whether they need to select it or drop it. This can be a time-consuming process, and the first time you try it, it can really be tough. But as you grow to know your collection and how item numbers work, this gets much easier. Also, since you can drop items anytime, always try to err on the side of adding too much. Don't let the Zero-Based Review and Item Selection Update stress you out. No one is going to have a finely tuned collection straight out of the gates.

Keep in mind, however, that once you drop something, you can't add it back until the next Annual Item Selection Cycle. So be careful. Don't rush to drop everything during that one-month period. Let your Zero-Based Review and update cycle last all year. Work through each segment of the collection systematically. Drop things as you find them and make a list of things to add as you go. This is also the time to look for things you get in print that you may want to transition to electronic; but *do not* drop the print until you can add the electronic title. Depending on how the access to individual resources works, you may end up with a gap in the collection, and you want to avoid that if you can. Just because there is a month designated for the update cycle doesn't mean you have to limit your work to that particular month.

Also, be careful that you don't accidentally drop an item from the core collection. The core collection is a list of resources that the FDLP has identified as important for all depository libraries. So, you need to make sure those are selected. The nice thing is that the majority of these items are available in electronic formats. If something is really important, you can usually select both print and electronic. For instance, I chose to receive the *Catalog of Federal Domestic Assistance* in both formats since, in parts of rural Georgia, the Internet is not always right at hand. The print copy went into the reference collection. If you select electronic only for any of the core collection, make sure the documents get into the catalog or create a Web page linking out to them. The FDLP and GPO really like to see those documents highlighted.

SuDocs

Adjusting to the Superintendent of Documents classification scheme can be frustrating at first, but it really makes a lot sense once you get used to using it. There are some great tutorials available on the Internet. Do a Google search for "SuDoc" to get started. The system is based on the current organization of the government. As a result, documents must sometimes be reclassified, and sometimes documents from the same issuing agency may be located in different parts of the system.

The overall scheme behind the SuDoc system is to group items with the same government author together and then together with that main author's subordinate organizations. The main author is signaled by the beginning letters of the stem, and then the subordinate agencies get a number. For instance, the Department of Agriculture uses the letter A. The Forest Service, which is under the Department of Agriculture, is assigned the number 13. Thus, items emanating from the Forest Service are assigned the SuDoc stem A 13. The next designation is the series. The number 1 is assigned to annual reports, so the annual report for the Forest Service would be A 13:1. Designations can further break down categories, but this is generally how it works. One thing to remember is that SuDoc is not a decimal point system. The number after the point is a whole number so D 1.3 comes before D 1.12.

The portion of the call number before the colon is the stem and the portion after the colon is the book number. Each publication and issue is given a book number, depending on the type of publication, such as serials, numbered and unnumbered monographs, and so on. For serials, for example, the number is usually the volume and issue number. So, Volume 10, Issue No. 2 of *Airman* would look like this: D 301.60: 10/2.

To help you watch for classification and cataloging changes, the FDLP issues the *Technical Supplement to the Administrative Notes* (see Appendix C). The list can be pretty long, so if you have to pass this list to someone else to make the cataloging changes, you may want to go through the list and mark the ones that need to be changed. It is always a plus when you can make something easier for someone and it is generally appreciated. Going through the list yourself also helps you keep up with any changes.

Cataloging and Bibliographic Control

The single best thing you can do to increase visibility and usage is to get those document records into your local catalog. Depending on your situation, this can be an easy thing or one of the most difficult in relation to other depository coordinator responsibilities. In my case, the documents associate and I cataloged everything ourselves, so things got into the catalog very quickly. If you do not have any access to the catalog, you are totally at the mercy of the catalogers, and generally they are going to catalog documents last. If you are in the least bit interested in cataloging, try your hand at cataloging the documents yourself.

If cataloging just isn't in your future, use other strategies to get documents cataloged. Remember the advice to make others' jobs as easy as possible. When you get new documents, print off the OCLC record and put it with the document. That way, you have already identified the record the catalogers need, and all they will have to do is use that OCLC number to pull it up and then download it. Do everything you can to make it as easy as possible for the catalogers to get the documents into the system. For the most part, GPO catalogers get items cataloged and into OCLC pretty quickly, so it is just a matter of copy cataloging.

Another option is to use commercial catalog record vendors. There are two that supply records for government publications. Using your profile of item numbers, the vendor will collect the records you need and dump them in the catalog for you. Then, when you get the physical items, all you have to do is attach a barcode. These vendors will also create temporary records for items that the GPO hasn't gotten cataloged yet.

There are pros and cons for using a commercial vendor. First, these vendors are not cheap, and they don't necessarily take all the work off your plate. You have to verify that the records that were loaded were for items you actually received. So, you have to go in and look at the records anyway and remove the ones you don't need. And if you have an item and no record, you have to go download that record. Another problem is tracking the temporary records. What is supposed to happen is that when a complete record becomes available, the vendor downloads it and that permanent record is supposed to overlay onto the temp record so that any local changes, like location or barcode number, remain. Sometimes this works and sometimes it doesn't. So, you will still be going into the catalog and doing maintenance on the records. However, there are all kinds of levels of vendor service. You do not have to buy the whole package. For instance, there are services you can purchase that just load electronic records from your profile. But be aware that someone will still have to check through all the records.

The usefulness of these services really depends on your situation. If you are a big library, like a regional, or have problems getting things cataloged, it may make sense to use a vendor. If you are a smaller library and have a good relationship with the cataloger, going without the vendor may make more sense. Just make sure the technical services department knows what is expected of it and that you are as helpful as possible.

Processing

Processing is another area that usually falls within the domain of technical services. In most operations, however, the government documents folks do everything they can before sending the documents to another department. Each item received, regardless of format, must be stamped with a GPO property stamp that includes the date. Everything else, again, must be equal to what the rest of the collection receives.

Putting security strips on materials is another issue. Those little pieces of sticky metal are expensive. Only put a security strip on an item if the replacement cost warrants one. For instance, we stripped monographs but not pamphlets. We didn't strip individual newsletters either, but we did strip the notebook they were housed in. Barcoding, however, is different. While we didn't strip individual newsletter or pamphlets, each one did get a barcode and did get cataloged. The FDLP requires piece-level holdings records for all tangible items. In other words, each individual physical item you receive must be cataloged. For newsletters and serials, you simply add the new issue onto the record you already have. For pamphlets, you generally have to download a whole new record.

Preservation

For tangible items, again, preservation concerns should follow right along with what is done for the commercial collection. According to the GPO, all materials should be housed in a stable environment, which means the temperature and humidity are regulated, and maps and microfiche are stored in sturdy and acid-free cases. Here is where your Binding Policy comes into play. Use the library's commercial collection as a guide and bind similar materials. Most of the time libraries send materials out to the bindery once a month. When I realized we needed this policy, I made an appointment with the person in charge of the library's binding, and we decided I would bring down a few things each month. It worked out really well.

Microfiche provides an interesting preservation concern. GPO microfiche uses the diazo process, which uses ultraviolet light, chemical, and ammonia vapor to create an image on translucent paper. Diazo microfiche often fades and is not considered a medium for archival preservation. Keep all staples and rubber bands away from the diazo microfiche, and don't store diazo fiche with any other kind of fiche. The different chemicals could damage the fiche.[1]

For electronic resources, preservation is new ground and more ambiguous. The GPO is interested in forming partnerships with libraries to investigate different electronic preservation methods. One such method is LOCKSS (Lots of Copies Keeps Stuff Safe). Developed by Stanford University, LOCKSS allows libraries, with the permission of the publisher, to download, preserve, and offer access to electronic documents. LOCKSS is an open source peer-to-peer system that runs on OpenBSD, a Unix-like operating system, on an ordinary computer.[2] The GPO is exploring using LOCKSS to comply with the part of Title 44 that charges it with providing permanent access to government information. The pilot project, launched in June 2005, involved 18 libraries associated with colleges or universities, Deutsche Bibliothek, and the National Agriculture Library.[3] The second phase of the project will involve three "real world scenarios" designed to test what was implemented in the pilot project.[4]

There are also some really interesting efforts to preserve and digitize state documents that would be very good models for federal projects. The Digital Library of Georgia, for instance, has worked to digitize a number of state government publications using programs it developed, while the New Mexico State Library developed a state government digitization project using OCLC's Digital Archive Service. With all the buzz surrounding Institutional Repositories and digital archiving these days, there are numerous opportunities and ways for documents librarians to do what they do best—preserve and provide access to federal information.

Regardless of format, however, the GPO and FDLP realize that library budgets are limited and offer very good guidelines for prioritizing preservation efforts. Among factors that can influence preservation decisions are the item's value as an artifact, high usage, availability in other libraries or other formats, its current condition, and cost effectiveness. For instance, you wouldn't want to necessarily spend a lot of money on an item that most libraries have and is online, but you may want to take steps to preserve a rare historical document. If your shelving isn't 6 inches off the ground, I doubt any library can afford to remedy that, but you can keep those rare documents off the lower shelves. Just do the best you can with what you have—making an effort and exercising due diligence will be appreciated.

Authentication and Version Control

This is another area that is new and different in the electronic environment. When items were only received in tangible format, proving where it came from and what edition was pretty straightforward. But the Internet has changed all that. The GPO is also charged with ensuring that government information is authentic and current under Title

44. Anyone can create a Web page and there have been some pretty sophisticated spoofs of official government Web sites. Finding a way to "mark" official government publications in the electronic environment has proven to be a challenge.

Currently, the GPO is involved in a major authentication initiative that will "assure users that the information made available by GPO is official and authentic and that trust relationships exist between all participants in electronic transactions."[5] The initiative will use Public Key Infrastructure (PKI) technology so that the agencies can digitally sign the PDF documents. This technology will protect documents against being altered and provide users with a way to determine if an electronic document is an official governmental publication.

Version control is another issue. Once a publication is issued in print, any changes come as an erratum or in the form of a new edition. In the electronic world, publishing agencies can go in and change publications and update them quickly and easily. So, even though the document is still there, its previous edition is gone forever. The issue of versioning has become so convoluted that Bruce James, the Public Printer, goes as far as to question what a version is in today's electronic world, stating "Today, with agencies able to update databases all day long, the question becomes, what is a version?" and further "What becomes a savable version of government information?"[6] In order to address this issue, the GPO has developed the Future Digital System (FDsys), mentioned briefly in Chapter 3, "The Modern GPO and FDLP," which will "manage, preserve, provide version control and access to, and disseminate authentic Government information."[7] The FDsys's first stage is scheduled to go live in 2007.

Conclusion

Since most depository librarians come from public services, the realm of technical services may very well be one of the hardest areas of documents librarianship to get a good handle on. But it is also where much of the action is today. The regulation, acquisition, preservation, and management of electronic resources are where all the new technologies and experiments are. This means that no matter where you go from here, working in this context with electronic documents will serve you well. Don't fear the technology; master it!

From the Trenches

- Learn as much as you can about technical services.

- Make other folks' jobs as easy as possible.

- You must place a GPO property stamp on every tangible item you receive.

- You must maintain holdings down to the piece level.

- Use security strips wisely.

- Make sure the documents collection's preservation standards are at least equal to that of the commercial collection.

- Get it in the catalog any way you can!

Endnotes

1. Library Programs Service, Superintendent of Documents, *Federal Depository Library Manual* (Washington, D.C.: U.S. Government Printing Office, 1993). Available online at www.access.gpo.gov/su_docs/fdlp/pubs/fdlm/93fdlm.html.
2. LOCKSS Homepage. Available online at www.lockss.org.
3. Government Printing Office, "GPO LOCKSS Pilot Project." Available online at www.access.gpo.gov/su_docs/fdlp/lockss/.
4. "Depository Library Council Update, April 2006." Available online at www.access.gpo.gov/su_docs/fdlp/pubs/proceedings/06spring/gpo_update_spring06.pdf.
5. "Depository Library Council Update, April 2006."
6. Aliya Sternstein, Mission Impossible: Printing in the Digital Age, Federal Computer Week, January 23, 2006. Available online at www.fcw.com/article 92034-01-23-06.
7. "Depository Library Council Update, April 2006." Available online at www.access.gpo.gov/su_docs/fdlp/pubs/proceedings/06spring/gpo_update_spring06.pdf.

The Burning Question Answered

If being a government documents librarian was so great, why did I leave my position in Georgia? Leaving Georgia had nothing to do with government documents at all. In fact, it was an outgrowth of working with documents that led me to health sciences. Working with Department of Health resources and PubMed piqued my interest. Plus, the documents collection was off probation and purring along. I need a challenge, I always have. And remember when I advised you to grab an opportunity when it presented itself? When I saw the job advertisement for Lister Hill, I grabbed it. So, I don't consider myself out of documents at all, just working with another facet of it.

Now remember, this isn't a comprehensive work on all things government documents, but it is intended to provide an introduction to managing a government documents collection and all the benefits it offers. So remember to take a look at the resources listed in the bibliography and Appendix A. I hope the book has generated your interest in government documents and librarianship. Please feel free to e-mail me with questions or comments at lennis@uab.edu.

Resources and Additional Readings

For those interested in a particular chapter, I've divided the materials into two categories. The items under "Resources" are tools or portions of tools specific to chapter content. The items under "Additional Readings" are for further discourse on a topic. For instance, the URL to GODORT is listed as resource, but *A History of the Government Documents Round Table* is listed as an additional reading. Some things may appear under more than one chapter because they are pertinent to the topic.

Chapter 1: Government Documents Librarianship: The Sky's the Limit

Resources

Cocklin, John and Linda B. Johnson. 2000. 1999 Bibliography on Documents Librarianship and Government Information. *DttP: Documents to the People* 28 (2): 65–68.

GODORT Government Information Technology Committee E-competencies. Available at www.ala.org/ala/godort/godort communities/gitco/ecomps.htm

Top 10 List for New Depository Coordinators on the FDLP Desktop, www.access.gpo.gov/su_docs/fdlp/mgt/top10.html

Additional Readings

Cross, Barbara Marston and John Richardson, Jr. "The Educational Preparation of Government Information Specialists." *Journal of Education for Library and Information Science.*

Ennis, Lisa A. 2003. "Management in the Middle: Life is Unfair." *Info Career Trends*: 1–3.

Gordon, Rachel Singer. 2003. *The Accidental Library Manager.* Medford, NJ: Information Today, Inc.

Kile, Barbara, Ridley R. Kessler, Jr., and Walter Newsome. 2004. "Experience Speaks: Thoughts on Documents Librarianship." *DttP: Documents to the People* 32 (1): 12–16.

Malone, Chuck. 1998. "Thinking Like a Government Documents Librarian." *Illinois Libraries* 80: 199–203.

Robinson, Judith Schiek. 2004. "We Are All Documents Librarians: Naturalizing the Next Generation." *DttP: Documents to the People* 32 (4): 22–24.

Shaw, James T. 2005. *How to be a Depository Library without Being a Depository Library: Adding Records for Electronic Government Documents to Our Catalog.* Joint Spring Meeting of the College and University Section and Technical Services Round Table of the Nebraska Library Association, Doane College, Crete, Nebraska.

Weatherly, C. Diann. 1996. A U.S. Government Publications Collection in a Non-Depository Research Library: A Case Study. *Journal of Government Information* 23 (4): 471–489.

Weatherly, C. Diann. 1997. *To Be or Not to Be a Depository: Answering the Questions and Envisioning a Brighter Future.* Proceedings of the 6th Annual Federal Depository Library Conference.

Yang, Zheng Ye (Lan). 2001. "An Assessment of Education and Training Needs for Government Documents Librarians in the United States." *Journal of Government Information* 28: 425–439.

Chapter 2: GPO and FDLP History: A Look Back Before Moving Forward

Resources

Depository Library Council on the FDLP Desktop, www.access.gpo.gov/su_docs/fdlp/council/

FDLP Desktop, www.access.gpo.gov/su_docs/fdlp/

FDLP Glossary on the FDLP Desktop, www.access.gpo.gov/su_docs/fdlp/tools/glossary.html

FirstGov, www.firstgov.gov

GPO Access, www.access.gpo.gov

GPO Homepage, www.gpo.gov

Title 44 U.S.C. on the FDLP Desktop, www.access.gpo.gov/su_docs/fdlp/pubs/title44/

Additional Readings

GPO, 2004 Annual Report.

GPO's Living History: Adelaide R. Hasse, www.access.gpo.gov/su_ docs/fdlp/history/hasse.html

Kling, Jr., Robert E. 1970. *The Government Printing Office*. New York: Praeger.

MacGilvray, Daniel R. "A Short History of the GPO." Available at www.access.gpo.gov/su_docs/fdlp/history/macgilvray.html

Chapter 3: The Modern GPO and FDLP: The Neo-Depository Era

Resources

Browse Topics, www.library.okstate.edu/govdocs/browsetopics/

The Federal Government Information Environment for the 21st Century: Towards a Vision Statement and Plan of Action for Federal Depository Libraries, Discussion Paper. Available at www.access. gpo.gov/su_docs/fdlp/pubs/dlc_vision_09_02_2005.pdf

Strategic Vision for the 21st Century, www.gpo.gov/congressional/ pdfs/04strategicplan.pdf

Additional Readings

FDsys Requirements Document v1.0, www.gpo.gov/projects/pdfs/ FDsys_RD_v1.0.pdf

FDsys Concept of Operations v2.0, www.gpo.gov/projects/pdfs/ FDsys_ConOps_v2.0.pdf

FDsys Phase 3 Summary, www.gpo.gov/projects/pdfs/Summary_ Phase3.pdf

Jacobs, James A., James R. Jacobs, and Shinjoung Yeo. 2005. "Government Information in the Digital Age: The Once and Future Federal Depository Library Program." *Journal of Academic Librarianship* 32 (3): 198–208.

Shuler, John. 2005. "The Political and Economic Future of Federal Depository Libraries." *Journal of Academic Librarianship* 31 (5): 377–382.

Chapter 4: FDLP Requirements: Dragons and Beasts

Resources

Electronic Federal Depository Library Manual (not yet published)
Library Programs Service. Superintendent of Documents. 1993. *Federal Depository Library Manual.* Washington, DC: U.S. Government Printing Office.
Library Programs Service. Superintendent of Documents. 2000. *Instructions to Depository Libraries.* Washington, DC: U.S. Government Printing Office.
Work Station Specifications, www.access.gpo.gov/su_docs/fdlp/computers/index.html

Additional Readings

Depository Library Council and DLC Operations Committee. Subcommittee on Attrition and Retention. 2002. *Suggested Responses to Frequently Cited Reasons for Leaving the Depository Library System.*
Kownslar, Edward. 1999. "Closing Down a Government Documents Collection: The Experiences of Millsaps College." *Documents to the People* 27 (4): 11–12.
McKenzie, Elizabeth M., Robert E. Dugan, and Kristin Djorup. 2000. "Leaving the Federal Depository Library Program." *Journal of Academic Librarianship* 26 (4): 282–285.
Rawan, Atifa. 2003. A Virtual Depository: Arizona Project. Proceedings of the Annual Fall Depository Library Conference. Available at www.access.gpo.gov/su_docs/fdlp/pubs/proceedings/03pro_rawan.ppt.
Scheitle, Janet. 2005. Depository Library 301: Electronic Depository Manual. Proceedings of the Annual Fall Depository Library Conference & Council Meeting. Available at www.access.gpo.gov/su_docs/fdlp/pubs/proceedings/05fall/index.html/janet_scheitle_manual_oct05.ppt.

Chapter 5: Networking and Training: You Are Not Alone

Resources

American Association of Law Libraries, www.aallnet.org
American Library Association, www.ala.org

Ask a Question, gpo.custhelp.com/cgi-bin/gpo.cfg/php/enduser/ ask.php

DLC Vision Blog, dlcvisionoutline.blogspot.com

Future Digital System (FDsys) Blog, fdsys.blogspot.com

GODORT, www.ala.org/Template.cfm?Section=godort

Govdoc-L, govdoc-l.org

Govdoc-L Archives, docs.lib.duke.edu/federal/govdoc-l/search.html

How to Draft a State Plan on the FDLP Desktop, www.access.gpo.gov/ su_docs/fdlp/pubs/proceedings/98pro2.html

Knowledgebase on the FDLP Desktop, www.gpoaccess.gov/help/ index.html

MAGERT, magert.whoi.edu

Proceedings of the Federal Depository Library Conferences on the FDLP Desktop, www.access.gpo.gov/su_docs/fdlp/pubs/proceedings/ index.html

RSS Main page on the FDLP Desktop, www.gpoaccess.gov/rss

Regional Depository Librarians on the FDLP Desktop, www.access. gpo.gov/su_docs/fdlp/pubs/regionals2005.pdf

Special Library Association, www.sla.org

Welcome to GPOLISTSERV on the FDLP Desktop, listserv.access. gpo.gov

Additional Readings

Hernon, Peter, Harold C. Relyea, Robert E. Dugan, and Joan F. Cheverie. *United States Government Information: Policies and Sources.* Westport, CT: Libraries Unlimited, 2002.

Mills, Lois, Larry Romans, and Sandy Peterson. *A History of the Government Documents Round Table.* Bethesda, MD: LexisNexis Academic & Library Solutions, 2002. Available at sunsite.berkeley. edu/GODORT/GODORT_history_final.pdf.

Morehead, Joe. *Introduction to United States Government Information Sources,* 6th edition. Englewood, CO: Libraries Unlimited, 1999.

Smith, Diane H. *Management of Government Information Resources in Libraries,* Englewood, CO: Libraries Unlimited, 1993.

Chapter 6: Managing and Administering: The Big Picture

Resources

Biennial Survey of Depository Libraries on the FDLP Desktop, www.access.gpo.gov/su_docs/fdlp/bisurvey/index.html

FDLP Guidelines for Determining Superseded Materials on the FDLP Desktop, www.access.gpo.gov/su_docs/fdlp/coll-dev/supersede. html

Federal Bulletin Board, fedbbs.access.gpo.gov/fdlp01.htm

GODORT Handout Exchange, www.lib.umich.edu/govdocs/godort. html

GPO Contact on the FDLP Desktop, www.access.gpo.gov/su_docs/ fdlp/tools/contacts.html

Knowledge Base on the FDLP Desktop, www.gpoaccess.gov/help/ index.html

Policies on Depository Management on the FDLP Desktop, www. access.gpo.gov/su_docs/fdlp/mgt/index.html#policies

Self-Study and Inspection Information on the FDLP Desktop, www.access.gpo.gov/su_docs/fdlp/selfstudy/index.html

Shipping Lister on the FDLP Desktop, www.access.gpo.gov/su_docs/ fdlp/tools/sl/slister.html

Web Claim on the FDLP Desktop, www.access.gpo.gov/su_docs/fdlp/ tools/webclaim.html

Additional Readings

Ennis, Lisa A. 2003. "Management in the Middle: Life is Unfair." *Info Career Trends*: 1–3.

Ennis, Lisa A. 2003. "Saving a Collection from the Brink of Disaster, Or Life as a Chihuahua in a Rottweiler World." *DttP: Documents to the People* 31 (3/4): 36–37.

Chapter 7: Public Services Issues: Making the Government Documents Collection Sparkle

Resources

Ben's Guide to U.S. Government Documents for Kids, bensguide. gpo.gov

FDLP Graphics on the FDLP Desktop, www.access.gpo.gov/su_docs/ fdlp/pr/graphics.html

FDLP Internet Use Policy Guidelines on the FDLP Desktop, www.access.gpo.gov/su_docs/fdlp/mgt/iupolicy.html

Federal Depository Library Program Promotion Plan on the FDLP Desktop, April 2002, www.access.gpo.gov/su_docs/fdlp/pr/ promo_plan.pdf

GODORT Handout Exchange, www.lib.umich.edu/govdocs/godort. html

Government Information Model Web Page Template on the FDLP Desktop, www.ala.org/ala/godort/godortcommunities/gitco/ index.htm

Order Depository Materials on the FDLP Desktop, www.access. gpo.gov/su_docs/fdlp/pr/order.html

Promoting Depository Collections and Services on the FDLP Desktop, www.access.gpo.gov/su_docs/fdlp/pr/index.html

Workstation Specifications on the FDLP Desktop at www.access. gpo.gov/su_docs/fdlp/computers/index.html

Additional Readings

Cheney, Debora. "Government Information Reference Service: New Roles and Models for the Post-Depository Era." *DttP: Documents to the People* 32 (3) (Fall 2004): 32–37.

Downie, Judith A. "Integrating Government Documents into Information Literacy Instruction, Part II." *DttP: Documents to the People* 32 (4) (Winter 2004): 17–22.

Downie, Judith A. "The Current Information Literacy Instruction Environment for Government Documents (pt I)." *DttP: Documents to the People* 32 (2) (Summer 2004): 36–39.

Ennis, Lisa A., "Opportunistic Documents Promotion." *Administrative Notes: Newsletter of the FDLP.* 24 (7) (June 15, 2003): 25–26.

Morehead, Joe. *Introduction to United States Government Information Sources,* 6th edition. Englewood, CO: Libraries Unlimited, 1999.

Siess, Judith. *The Visible Librarian: Asserting Your Value through Marketing and Advocacy.* Chicago, American Library Association, 2003.

Wilhite, Jeffrey M. "Internet Versus Live: Assessment of Government Documents Bibliographic Instruction." *Journal of Government Information* 30 (2004): 561–574.

Chapter 8: Technical Services Issues: The Devil Is In the Details

Resources

Administrative Notes Technical Supplement on the FDLP Desktop, www.access.gpo.gov/su_docs/fdlp/pubs/techsup/index.html

Basic Collection on the FDLP Desktop, www.access.gpo.gov/su_docs/fdlp/coll-dev/basic-01.html

Collection Development on the FDLP Desktop, www.access.gpo.gov/su_docs/fdlp/coll-dev/index.html

Digital Documents Program Permanent Public Access through the New Mexico State Library, www.stlib.state.nm.us/DigitalArchive.htm

Digital Library of Georgia, dlg.galileo.usg.edu

Documents Data Miner, govdoc.wichita.edu/ddm/GdocFrames.asp

An Explanation of the Superintendent of Documents Classification System on the FDLP Desktop, www.access.gpo.gov/su_docs/fdlp/pubs/explain.html

Future Digital System, www.gpo.gov/projects/fdsys.htm

Future Digital System Blog, fdsys.blogspot.com

GPO LOCKSS Pilot Project on the FDLP Desktop, www.access.gpo.gov/su_docs/fdlp/lockss/

Item Amendment of Selections on the FDLP Desktop, www.gpo.gov/su_docs/fdlp/tools/amendment.html

Item Lister on the FDLP Desktop, www.access.gpo.gov/su_docs/fdlp/tools/itemlist.html

List of Classes on the FDLP Desktop, www.access.gpo.gov/su_docs/fdlp/pubs/loc/index.html

Lots of Copies Keeps Stuff Safe, www.lockss.org

Additional Readings

Cataloging Branch, Library Programs Service. *Government Printing Office Cataloging Guidelines*, Fourth Edition. Washington, DC: GPO, 2002. Available at www.access.gpo.gov/su_docs/fdlp/cip/gpocatgu.doc.

Etkin, Cindy. "Franklin: Your Key to Government Information." Available at www.access.gpo.gov/su_docs/fdlp/cip/cindy_etkin_ franklin_online.pdf.

Malone, Chuck. "Thinking Like a Government Documents Librarian." *Illinois Libraries* 80 (Fall 1998): 199–203.

Biennial Survey

Taking a close look at the Biennial Survey, mentioned in Chapter 6, "Managing and Administering," is a good exercise for all librarians interested in government documents. Not only does the Biennial Survey provide an excellent look at the types of reports a depository coordinator can expect to complete, but it also can be a way to gauge what the FDLP believes is important and can provide hints about the direction the FDLP is heading. For instance, on the Biennial Survey Web page (www.access.gpo.gov/su_docs/fdlp/bisurvey/index.html) you can download the surveys and the survey results from 1997, 1999, 2001, 2003, and 2005. From just a glance, you can see how the questions have changed over time to reflect more of an emphasis on electronic documents.

Biennial Survey of Depository Libraries, 2005

I have reviewed my library's profile information on the previous page, and:
  ○ All the information is correct.
  ○ Some of the information is incorrect, and the corrections were submitted to GPO using the Depository Directory Form on the previous page.

Depository library number:
  [   ]

Enter your INTERNAL password:
  [   ]

Enter your email address:
  [   ]

  (Please enter your e-mail address to receive confirmation of your Biennial Survey response)

1a. Do you want to remain in the Federal Depository Library Program?
  ○ Yes
  ○ No

  If you answered "No," please contact the GPO Customer Contact Center and choose "Federal Depository Libraries" as the category and "Depository Designation Status" as the subcategory.

1b. Is the library in the process of reconsidering depository status?
  ○ Yes
  ○ No

COLLECTION DEVELOPMENT

2. How many cataloged and uncataloged items are in your library system? Include Federal depository and non-depository materials, all formats, and collections and libraries under the purview of your library director.
  ○ less than 250,000
  ○ 250,000 - 1,000,000
  ○ more than 1,000,000

3. Depository's selection rate (as a percentage) from **Item Lister**?
  [▼]

  (Round off to higher whole number, e.g., 28.91 is rounded to 29.)

4. Do you have a **written** collection development policy for U.S. Government depository documents?

○ **YES** and revised within the last five years?
○ **YES** but **NOT** revised within the last five years?
○ **NO**

5. Are Federal depository documents integrated into the library's main collection?
   ○ **All**
   ○ **Most**
   ○ **Some**
   ○ **None**

5a. Are any Federal depository documents housed in a location separate from the majority of the depository collection (e.g., titles sent to reference, periodicals, etc.)?
   ○ Yes
   ○ No

5b. If YES, what percentage do you estimate is in remote storage?
(for none, choose 0)
   [▼]

6. Are you substituting any official online resources
(http://www.access.gpo.gov/su_docs/fdlp/coll-dev/subguide.html) for tangible depository materials?
   ○ Yes
   ○ No

BIBLIOGRAPHIC CONTROL

7. Do you provide piece-level records for **ALL** depository receipts?
   ○ Yes
   ○ No

8. Is your shelflist for the depository collection (Check all that apply):
   ☐ Part of an integrated library system
   ☐ PC-based
   ☐ Card-based
   ☐ Other (specify) [   ]

9. Is the processing of depository receipts integrated into the processing unit for other library materials?
   ○ Yes
   ○ No

MAINTENANCE

10. Are written binding and replacement policies in place for depository materials?
   ○ Yes
   ○ No

11. Does the library have a disaster plan in which the Federal depository collection is included?
   ○ Yes
   ○ No

12. The depository collection is weeded:
  ○ **Regularly**
  ○ **Irregularly**
  ○ **Never**

13. Are documents included in the library's major preservation and conservation activities (e.g., binding, encapsulating, materials moved to climate controlled areas)?
  ○ Yes
  ○ No

14. Is the majority of the print depository collection arranged using the SuDocs classification?
  ○ Yes
  ○ No

HUMAN RESOURCES

15. Number of FTE (full time equivalencies) staff devoted to Federal depository operations (e.g., based on a 40-hour work week, if four librarians spend 100 hours per week on depository activities, report 2.5 FTE for librarians):
NOTE: For this question 15, please fill in **EACH** block below, even if only to answer 0.

15a. Librarians, Full Time Equivalent(FTE)

15b. Support Staff, Full Time Equivalent(FTE)

15c. Other (students, volunteers, etc.), Full Time Equivalent(FTE)

15d. Has your library's depository staffing decreased in recent years?
  ○ Yes
  ○ No

If the answer to 15d. above is YES, please answer the following (15e - 15h):

15e. Budget constraints are limiting staffing
  ○ True
  ○ False

15f. Cross training of staff allows us to function with less full time documents staff
  ○ True
  ○ False

15g. An increase in Web/electronic publications means we need less staff for processing and other related functions for tangible depository collections.
  ○ True
  ○ False

15h. Other. Specify _____

16. Is the depository operation an independently administered unit (i.e., responsible for procedures and policies)?
   ○ Yes
   ○ No

16a. If "No," with which area(s) is documents most closely associated?
   ☐ Acquisitions
   ☐ Administration
   ☐ Cataloging
   ☐ Reference
   ☐ Special Collections
   ☐ Subject Collection (e.g., business, social sciences)
   ☐ Other ☐

16b. Was your library's documents department consolidated with other library departments?
   ○ Yes
   ○ No

16c. If Yes to 16b. above, check all the reasons that apply:
   ☐ Buget/staffing constraints moved us to consolidate departments in the library.
   ☐ We consolidated documents into another areas so as to spread documents expertise across a broader cross section of the library staff.
   ☐ The increasing Web/electronic nature of the FDLP meant we felt we didn't need a seperate document unit but could sucessfully incorporate it into another library department.
   ☐ Other. Specify ☐

17. Does the library administration budget for attendance at meetings and continuing education activities for professional staff? (Check all that apply)
   ☐ Local
   ☐ State
   ☐ National
   ☐ Regional
   ☐ Does not support
   ☐ Other (specify) ☐

18. Does the library administration budget for attendance at meetings and continuing education activities for support staff? (Check all that apply)
   ☐ Local
   ☐ State
   ☐ National
   ☐ Regional
   ☐ Does not support
   ☐ Other (specify) ☐

PHYSICAL FACILITIES

19. Since the 2003 Biennial Survey, has any construction, remodeling, or relocation affected the depository operation?
   ○ Yes
   ○ No

20. Are there any barriers to depository resources (print and electronic) for persons with disabilities?

    ○ **YES, to all resources**

    ○ **YES**, to some resources

    ○ **NO**

20a. If Yes, what specific barriers exist? Check/enter all that apply:

    □ Difficult access into the building (lack of or inadequate ramp, handicapped doors, etc.)

    □ Difficult Access to depository collection is the library, i.e. no elevator to documents collection(s)

    □ Stack aisles are too narrow for wheel chair access

    □ Insufficient or no computer workstations, at which FDLP materials can be accessed, that are adequate for wheelchair/handicapped access.

    □ Insufficient or no computer workstations, at which FDLP materials can be accessed, that have text reading and and/or other similar screen reading capabilities.

    □ Library computer screens/Web pages, etc., that can include depository materials, have 508 compliance problems (the Americans with Disabilities Act of 1990 (ADA) and Section 504 of the Rehabilitation Act of 1973).

    □ Other - Specify

21. At current selection rates and with regular collection maintenance, are there five years of growth room for the following depository formats ?

21a. .. Print

    ○ Yes

    ○ No

21b. .. Microfiche

    ○ Yes

    ○ No

21c. .. CD-ROMs/DVDs

    ○ Yes

    ○ No

21d. .. Maps

    ○ Yes

    ○ No

22a. Does the library have wireless (WiFi) access to the Internet?

    ○ Yes

    ○ No

22b. Does the library meet the "2005 Minimum Technical Requirements for Public Access Workstations in Federal Depository Libraries," (http://www.access.gpo.gov/su_docs/fdlp/computers/mtr.html) ?

    ○ Yes

    ○ No

23. Does the library have computer equipment for the physically challenged that uses assistive technologies (hardware or software) ?

○ Yes
○ No

24a. YES, Depository **CD-ROMs** are currently accessible via (Check all that apply):
☐ Stand alone workstation(s)
☐ Library-wide LAN
☐ Wide Area Network (WAN), beyond the library (i.e., campus wide)
☐ Internet
☐ Circulation to patrons

24b. NO Depository **CD-ROMs** are not available - **NOTE: DON'T** answer here if you answered YES above for 24a):
☐ We have CD-ROM capability, but we do not select depository CDs
☐ We select depository CDs, but we do not have CD-ROM capability
☐ We do not have CD-ROM capability nor do we select depository CDs

24c. YES, Depository **DVDs** are currently accessible via (Check all that apply):
☐ Stand alone workstation(s)
☐ Library-wide LAN
☐ Wide Area Network (WAN), beyond the library (i.e., campus wide)
☐ Internet
☐ Circulation to patrons

24d. NO Depository **DVDs** are not available - **NOTE: DON'T** answer here if you answered YES above for 24c):
☐ We have DVD capability, but we do not select depository DVDs
☐ We select depository DVDs, but we do not have DVD capability
☐ We do not have DVD capability nor do we select depository DVDs

PUBLIC SERVICE

25. How many hours per week is the library open? (Round off to next full hour.)
▢ ▾

26. How many hours per week is there professional level assistance (not necessarily by librarians) at the reference desk that services the depository collection? (Round off to next full hour.)
▢ ▾

27. Is there a service desk for the depository collection that is maintained separately from the library's main reference desk?
○ **YES,** and staffing (hours and level) comparable to that of the main reference desk
○ **YES, but** staffing (hours and level) **not** comparable to that of the main reference desk
○ **NO**

28. Does your library have a written access policy for the depository collection?
○ Yes
○ No

28a. Does your library require an ID to:
☐ Enter the library
☐ Use depository documents

☐ Neither of the above

29. Does your library have a written policy regarding public services for Government information in electronic formats?
(http://www.access.gpo.gov/su_docs/fdlp/mgt/pseguide.html)
   ○ Yes
   ○ No

30a. Does your library have a written policy for FDLP Internet use?
(http://www.access.gpo.gov/su_docs/fdlp/mgt/iupolicy.html)
   ○ Yes
   ○ No

30b. Does your library use filtering or blocking software on the public access workstations?
   ○ Yes
   ○ No

30c. Does your library have the ability to turn-off, or work around filtering/blocking software when patrons are doing research or need to use Federal Government information on the Web?
   ○ YES
   ○ NO
   ○ N/A

31. What type of catalog does your library have? (Check all that apply.)
   ☐ Card catalog
   ☐ Text-based online catalog
   ☐ Web-based online catalog
   ☐ Other (specify) [＿＿＿＿＿]

32. Are any U.S. depository documents included in the library's catalog?
   ○ Yes
   ○ No

32a. If "YES," What percent of **current** depository receipts are included in the library's catalog?
   [＿ ▼]

32b. If "YES," Do you use: (Check all that apply)
   ☐ Cataloging record loads
   ☐ Original/copy cataloging

33. What library system do you currently use?
   ○ Endeavor: Voyager
   ○ Ex Libris: Aleph
   ○ Geac: ADVANCE
   ○ Geac: PLUS
   ○ Geac: Vubis Smart
   ○ Innovative Interfaces, Inc. (III): Millennium
   ○ Innovative Interfaces, Inc. (III): Innopac
   ○ SirsiDynix: Dynix
   ○ SirsiDynix: Horizon

○ SirsiDynix: NOTIS LMS
○ SirsiDynix: Unicorn
○ The Library Corporation (TLC): Library.Solution
○ The Library Corporation (TLC): CARL.Solution
○ VTLS: Classic
○ VTLS: Virtua
○ None
○ Other (specify): [＿＿＿＿＿＿＿＿]

34. Are you planning to migrate to a new system within the next two years?
○ Yes
○ No

35. Are records for Internet-accessible electronic Federal Government information products included in your library's catalog?
(Select ONE best answer)
○ **YES**, and interface supports active hyperlinking capability
○ **YES**, though multiple interfaces are offered and not all support active hyperlinking capability
○ **YES**, BUT interface does not support active hyperlinking capability
○ **YES**, BUT the library made a policy decision not to link
○ **NO**

36. How are the library staff (depository and nondepository staff) regularly made aware of new Federal Government information products, services, and resources? (Check all that apply)
☐ Announcements from Administrative Notes routed
☐ Regular staff meetings
☐ E-mail
☐ Blog(s)[i.e. see http://fdsys.blogspot.com and http://dlcvisionoutline.blogspot.com]
☐ RSS [defintion]
☐ Intranet
☐ Demonstrations
☐ Help guides created
☐ Hands-on training sessions
☐ No regular program
☐ Other (specify) [＿＿＿＿＿＿＿]

37. Is the library's catalog available via (Check all that apply):
☐ Dial-in access
☐ Internet
☐ Network with other libraries
☐ Not applicable

38. The library's promotion (e.g., flyers, newspaper articles, etc.) of the depository to the general public can best be described as:
○ Active, on-going promotion to the general public
○ Infrequent promotion to the general public
○ No promotion to the general public

39. On average, how many incidents of use are there of the depository collections or services each week (including all incidents of use, i.e., in person, phone, fax, e-mail, PURL referral count, etc., but NOT Web site hit count)? You may choose a typical week to sample. This refers to the number of people using depository materials, not the number of people who enter the library.

| ▼ |

39a. Has the library signed up for the Statistical Information Request from GPO? This report allows your library to obtain statistical data on on the number of hits to GPO Access from your library OPAC (see http://www.access.gpo.gov/su_docs/fdlp/tools/ldirect.html#2).
　○ Yes
　○ No

40. Has your library conducted user surveys or other studies to determine the quality of depository services?
　○ Yes
　○ No

41. Does your library receive Federal funds for technology related purposes? (Check all that apply)
　☐ LSTA
　☐ IMLS
　☐ ESEA
　☐ N/A - Do NOT receive the above funds
　☐ Other (specify) |

COOPERATIVE EFFORTS

42. Is your Federal depository operation governed by a State Plan for providing government information services, including such elements as interlibrary cooperation, advisory group, coordination of training, etc?
　○ **YES**, and the Plan has been revised within the last five years.
　○ **YES**, BUT the Plan has NOT been revised within the last five years.
　○ **Don't know**
　○ **NO**

43. Do you use the **FDLP Desktop**?
(http://www.access.gpo.gov/su_docs/fdlp/index.html)
　○ **YES**
　○ **NO**, Did not know about it
　○ **NO**, Know about, but not how to use it
　○ **NO**, Not useful -- the subject matter or service is not something that is needed in my day-to-day library work.
　○ **NO**, Not useful -- it may be a useful service, but I found it too difficult to use, time consuming, or too confusing to use.
　○ **NO**, Not useful -- other. Specify: |

44. Do you use the **CRM System/GPO Customer Contact Center Help Service**?
(http://www.gpoaccess.gov/help/index.html)
　○ **YES**
　○ **NO**, Did not know about it
　○ **NO**, Know about, but not how to use it
　○ **NO**, Not useful -- the subject matter or service is not something that is needed in my

day-to-day library work.

○ **NO**, Not useful -- it may be a useful service, but I found it too difficult to use, time consuming, or too confusing to use.

○ **NO**, Not useful -- other. Specify: [   ]

45. Do you use the **Documents Data Miner II**?
(http://govdoc.wichita.edu/ddm2/)

○ **YES**

○ **NO**, Did not know about it

○ **NO**, Know about, but not how to use it

○ **NO**, Not useful -- the subject matter or service is not something that is needed in my day-to-day library work.

○ **NO**, Not useful -- it may be a useful service, but I found it too difficult to use, time consuming, or too confusing to use.

○ **NO**, Not useful -- other. Specify: [   ]

46. Do you use the **Resources for Federal Depository Library Directors**?
(http://www.access.gpo.gov/su_docs/fdlp/directors/index.html)

○ **YES**

○ **NO**, Did not know about it

○ **NO**, Know about, but not how to use it

○ **NO**, Not useful -- the subject matter or service is not something that is needed in my day-to-day library work.

○ **NO**, Not useful -- it may be a useful service, but I found it too difficult to use, time consuming, or too confusing to use.

○ **NO**, Not useful -- other. Specify: [   ]

47. Do you use the **Enhanced Shipping List Service**?
(http://www.access.gpo.gov/su_docs/fdlp/tools/sl/index.html)

○ **YES**

○ **NO**, Did not know about it

○ **NO**, Know about, but not how to use it

○ **NO**, Not useful -- the subject matter or service is not something that is needed in my day-to-day library work.

○ **NO**, Not useful -- it may be a useful service, but I found it too difficult to use, time consuming, or too confusing to use.

○ **NO**, Not useful -- other. Specify: [   ]

48. Do you use the **Federal Bulletin Board**?
(http://fedbbs.access.gpo.gov/)

○ **YES**

○ **NO**, Did not know about it

○ **NO**, Know about, but not how to use it

○ **NO**, Not useful -- the subject matter or service is not something that is needed in my day-to-day library work.

○ **NO**, Not useful -- it may be a useful service, but I found it too difficult to use, time consuming, or too confusing to use.

○ **NO**, Not useful -- other. Specify: [   ]

49. Do you use the **New Electronic Titles (NET)**?
(http://www.access.gpo.gov/su_docs/locators/net/index.html)
    ○ **YES**
    ○ **NO**, Did not know about it
    ○ **NO**, Know about, but not how to use it
    ○ **NO**, Not useful -- the subject matter or service is not something that is needed in my day-to-day library work.
    ○ **NO**, Not useful -- it may be a useful service, but I found it too difficult to use, time consuming, or too confusing to use.
    ○ **NO**, Not useful -- other. Specify: [ ]

50. Do you use the **Government Information Locator Service (GILS) via GPO Access**?
(http://www.access.gpo.gov/su_docs/gils/index.html)
    ○ **YES**
    ○ **NO**, Did not know about it
    ○ **NO**, Know about, but not how to use it
    ○ **NO**, Not useful -- the subject matter or service is not something that is needed in my day-to-day library work.
    ○ **NO**, Not useful -- it may be a useful service, but I found it too difficult to use, time consuming, or too confusing to use.
    ○ **NO**, Not useful -- other. Specify: [ ]

51. Do you use the **GPO Access Databases**?
(http://www.gpoaccess.gov/multidb.html)
    ○ **YES**
    ○ **NO**, Did not know about it
    ○ **NO**, Know about, but not how to use it
    ○ **NO**, Not useful -- the subject matter or service is not something that is needed in my day-to-day library work.
    ○ **NO**, Not useful -- it may be a useful service, but I found it too difficult to use, time consuming, or too confusing to use.
    ○ **NO**, Not useful -- other. Specify: [ ]

52. Do you use the **Catalog of U.S. Government Publications (CGP)**?
(http://www.gpoaccess.gov/cgp/index.html)
    ○ **YES**
    ○ **NO**, Did not know about it
    ○ **NO**, Know about, but not how to use it
    ○ **NO**, Not useful -- the subject matter or service is not something that is needed in my day-to-day library work.
    ○ **NO**, Not useful -- it may be a useful service, but I found it too difficult to use, time consuming, or too confusing to use.
    ○ **NO**, Not useful -- other. Specify: [ ]

53. Do you use the **Browse Topics**?
(http://www.gpoaccess.gov/topics/index.html)
    ○ **YES**
    ○ **NO**, Did not know about it
    ○ **NO**, Know about, but not how to use it

◌ **NO**, Not useful -- the subject matter or service is not something that is needed in my day-to-day library work.

◌ **NO**, Not useful -- it may be a useful service, but I found it too difficult to use, time consuming, or too confusing to use.

◌ **NO**, Not useful -- other. Specify: [   ]

54. Do you use the **Federal Agency Internet Sites**?
(http://www.gpoaccess.gov/agencies.html)

◌ **YES**

◌ **NO**, Did not know about it

◌ **NO**, Know about, but not how to use it

◌ **NO**, Not useful -- the subject matter or service is not something that is needed in my day-to-day library work.

◌ **NO**, Not useful -- it may be a useful service, but I found it too difficult to use, time consuming, or too confusing to use.

◌ **NO**, Not useful -- other. Specify: [   ]

55. Do you use the **U.S. Government Online Bookstore**?
(http://bookstore.gpo.gov/)

◌ **YES**

◌ **NO**, Did not know about it

◌ **NO**, Know about, but not how to use it

◌ **NO**, Not useful -- the subject matter or service is not something that is needed in my day-to-day library work.

◌ **NO**, Not useful -- it may be a useful service, but I found it too difficult to use, time consuming, or too confusing to use.

◌ **NO**, Not useful -- other. Specify: [   ]

56. Do you use the **Needs and Offers List**?
(http://www.access.gpo.gov/su_docs/fdlp/tools/needs_of/index.html)

◌ **YES**

◌ **NO**, Did not know about it

◌ **NO**, Know about, but not how to use it

◌ **NO**, Not useful -- the subject matter or service is not something that is needed in my day-to-day library work.

◌ **NO**, Not useful -- it may be a useful service, but I found it too difficult to use, time consuming, or too confusing to use.

◌ **NO**, Not useful -- other. Specify: [   ]

57. Do you use the **Ben's Guide to U.S. Government**?
(http://bensguide.gpo.gov)

◌ **YES**

◌ **NO**, Did not know about it

◌ **NO**, Know about, but not how to use it

◌ **NO**, Not useful -- the subject matter or service is not something that is needed in my day-to-day library work.

◌ **NO**, Not useful -- it may be a useful service, but I found it too difficult to use, time consuming, or too confusing to use.

◌ **NO**, Not useful -- other. Specify: [   ]

58. Do you use the **FDLP Announcement Service (FDLP-L)**?
(http://www.access.gpo.gov/su_docs/fdlp/tools/fdlplist.html)
  ○ **YES**
  ○ **NO**, Did not know about it
  ○ **NO**, Know about, but not how to use it
  ○ **NO**, Not useful -- the subject matter or service is not something that is needed in my day-to-day library work.
  ○ **NO**, Not useful -- it may be a useful service, but I found it too difficult to use, time consuming, or too confusing to use.
  ○ **NO**, Not useful -- other. Specify: [   ]

59. Do you use the **Free Depository Library Promotional Materials Order Form**?
(http://www.access.gpo.gov/su_docs/fdlp/pr/order.html)
  ○ **YES**
  ○ **NO**, Did not know about it
  ○ **NO**, Know about, but not how to use it
  ○ **NO**, Not useful -- the subject matter or service is not something that is needed in my day-to-day library work.
  ○ **NO**, Not useful -- it may be a useful service, but I found it too difficult to use, time consuming, or too confusing to use.
  ○ **NO**, Not useful -- other. Specify: [   ]

60. Does your library director subscribe to the **Directors Announcement Service (FDL-DIRECTORS-L)**?
(http://listserv.access.gpo.gov/archives/fdl-directors-l.html)
  ○ **YES**
  ○ **NO**, Did not know about it
  ○ **NO**, Know about, but not how to use it
  ○ **NO**, Not useful -- the subject matter or service is not something that is needed in my day-to-day library work.
  ○ **NO**, Not useful -- it may be a useful service, but I found it too difficult to use, time consuming, or too confusing to use.
  ○ **NO**, Not useful -- other. Specify: [   ]

TRAINING

Please indicate your level of interest in GPO provided or facilitated training in the following areas:

61a. Disaster planning
  [▼]

61b. Depository operations (processing shipments, collection development strategies and tools, etc.)
  [▼]

61c. Marketing/promotion
  [▼]

61c1. Depository Anniversary Celebrations
  [▼]

61c2. Library of the Year

[_____ ▼]

61c3. Marketing your depository library at the local level

[_____ ▼]

61d. GPO Access

[_____ ▼]

61e. Ben's Guide

[_____ ▼]

61f. FDLP Desktop

[_____ ▼]

61g. OPAC (Online Public Access Catalog - Franklin)

[_____ ▼]

61h. How to conduct user surveys

[_____ ▼]

61i. Grant opportunities/how to apply for grants

[_____ ▼]

61j. GPO Online Help

[_____ ▼]

61k. STAT-USA/USA Trade Online

[_____ ▼]

61l. Census materials

[_____ ▼]

61m. Geographic Information System (GIS)

[_____ ▼]

61n. Other
    ○ None
    ○ Specify: [_____]

DIGITALIZATION PROJECTS

62. Is your library currently involved in document digitization projects?
    ○ Yes
    ○ No

62a. If yes, what titles or which agencies' publications are you digitizing?
[_____]

62b. Are you using digitization specifications for:
    ○ Preservation level

⊙ Access level
⊙ Both

Definitions:
1. *preservation level:* Creation of preservation copies, which are copies that maintain all the characteristics of the original publication, from which true copies may be made. An example of a file format used for preservation masters is a TIFF file.
2. *access level:* Creation of access (or service) copies, which are digital publications whose characteristics are designed for ease or speed of access rather than preservation. An example of a file format for access copies is a screen-optimized PDF file.

62c. Do you offer unrestricted free use of your digitized collection to the general public?
⊙ Yes
⊙ No

62d. Are your digitized collections catalogued?
⊙ Yes
⊙ No

62e. If YES to 62d above, are these digitized collections catalog records available in a bibliographic utility? (indicate all that apply)
☐ YES, in OCLC
☐ YES, in RLIN
☐ YES, other (specify): [＿＿＿＿＿＿＿＿]
☐ NO
☐ Not applicable

63a. Does your depository participate in virtual reference services?
⊙ Yes
⊙ No

63b. Would you be interested in participating in a virtual reference service if it was administered by or through GPO?
⊙ Yes
⊙ No

64a1. What is the level of interest for your library for Spanish language FDLP materials?
[＿＿＿＿＿＿＿ ▼]

64b1. What is the level of interest for your library for FDLP materials in other languages?
[＿＿＿＿＿＿＿ ▼]

64b2. Please specify what languages you have an interest in.
☐ Amharic
☐ Arabic
☐ Armenian
☐ Bengali
☐ Bulgarian
☐ Cambodian
☐ Catalan

☐ Chinese
☐ Czech
☐ Dutch
☐ English
☐ French
☐ German
☐ Greek
☐ Hindi
☐ Hungarian
☐ Iloko
☐ Italian
☐ Japanese
☐ Korean
☐ Laotian
☐ Magahi
☐ Newari
☐ Persian
☐ Polish
☐ Portugese
☐ Romanian
☐ Russian
☐ Serbian
☐ Slovak

64b3. Other language(s), specify:

65. My library systematically downloads, stores online publications identified from GPO Access or through GPO-created PURLs, and makes them accessible to the general public from local servers. This past year my library downloaded the following number of digital publication files (this does not include shipping lists, Web pages, or databases):

- ○ 0
- ○ 1-25
- ○ 26-100
- ○ 101-500
- ○ 501-1000
- ○ 1001-5000
- ○ more than 5000

66. My library is willing to receive Federal digital publication files on deposit from GPO, store them, and make them accessible to the general public from local servers. My library is willing to receive the following number of digital publication files per year (this does not include shipping lists, Web pages, or databases):

- ○ 0
- ○ 1-25
- ○ 26-100
- ○ 101-500
- ○ 501-1000
- ○ 1001-5000

    ○ more than 5000

REVIEW AND APPROVAL

67. Declaration of review and approval.

    □ I herby certify that the library director or approving official has reviewed and approved this submission of the 2005 Biennial Survey for my library. In addition, a copy of this Survey submission will be e-mailed to the library director or approving official.

68a. Name of approving official

68b. Title of approving official

68c. E-mail address of approving official

68d. Phone number of approving official

submit

Administrative Notes:
Technical Supplement (ANTS)

The *Technical Supplement*, mentioned in Chapter 8, "Technical Services Issues," can be an intimidating list of cataloging and classification changes. An example of a *Technical Supplement* is included here for a quick look at how the newsletter is organized and the layout of the information. It is actually pretty easy to navigate and use despite any initial reaction folks have to the large charts of numbers, letters, and titles. There is also Web page with back issues located at www.access.gpo.gov/su_docs/fdlp/pubs/techsup/index.html.

ADMINISTRATIVE NOTES

Technical Supplement

| Vol. 13, no. 05-06 | GP 3.16/3-3:13/05-06 | May-June 30, 2006 |

Classification/Cataloging Update

May-June 2006				2006-03
CLASS	ITEM	SHIPPING LIST #	TITLE	STATUS
A 13.13:M 58	0085	Unknown	Middle Fork of the Salmon	Change class to: A 13.13: M 58/3.
A 13.13:M 58/2	0085	Unknown	Hunting on the Midewin National Grassland Prairie	Change class to: A 13.13: M 58/4.
A 92.53/57:997	0015-B-56	1999-0060E	1997 Census of Agriculture Geographic Area, V.1	Change class to: A 92.53/56:997.
A 92.53/57:997/V. 2/PT.1	0015-B-57	2000-0302-P	1997 Census of Agriculture, Agricultural Atlas of the United States, V.2, Pt.1	Change class to: A 92.54:997/V.2/PT.1.
AE 1.102:M 58/4	0569-B-02	2004-0093-P	Microfilm Publications, Pamphlet Describing M1904, Record Group 105	Change class to: AE 1.119: M1904. Correct item no. 0569-C-06.
C 55.2:ST 8/2000-2005	0250-E-02	EL only	NCEP Strategic Plan 2000-2005: Where America's Climate and Weather Services Begin	Change class to: C 55.2:ST 8/7/2000-2005.
C 55.402:AT 6/2	0192	2005-0014-S	Atlas of the Shallow-Water Benthic Habitats of American Samoa, Guam, and the Commonwealth of the Northern Mariana Islands, February 2005	Change class to: C 55.13/2:NOS NCCOS 8.
FEM 1.115:20010005 68	0216-A-22	EL only	Scrap and Shredded Tire Fires: Special Report	Change class to: FEM 1.115:093.
HE 20.3152:P 92/5/992-2	0507-G-02	1994-0665-M	President's Cancer Panel Special Commission on Breast Cancer, Transcript of Proceedings, October 23, 1993	Change class to: HE 20.3152:P 92/5-2/992-2.
HE 20.3152:P 92/5/993	0507-G-02	1994-0333-M	President's Cancer Panel Special Commission on Breast Cancer, Transcript of Proceedings, January 11-12, 1993	Change class to: HE 20.3152:P 92/5-2/993.
HE 20.3152:P 92/5/993-2	0507-G-02	1993-0610-P	President's Cancer Panel Special Commission on Breast Cancer, Transcript of Proceedings February 23, 1993	Change class to: HE 20.3152:P 92/5-2/993-2.

Classification/Cataloging Update

May-June 2006				2006-03
CLASS	*ITEM*	*SHIPPING LIST #*	*TITLE*	*STATUS*
HE 20.3152:P 92/5/993-3/V.1	*0507-G-02*	*1994-0452-M*	*President's Cancer Panel Special Commission on Breast Cancer, Transcript of Proceedings, March 18-19, 1993, V.1*	*Change class to: HE 20.3152:P 92/5-2/993-3/V.1.*
HE 20.3152:P 92/5/993-3/V.2	*0507-G-02*	*1994-0177-M*	*President's Cancer Panel Special Commission on Breast Cancer, Transcript of Proceedings, March 18-19, 1993, V.2*	*Change class to: HE 20.3152:P 92/5-2/993-3/V.2.*
HE 20.3152:P 92/5/993-4	*0507-G-02*	*1994-0400-M*	*President's Cancer Panel Special Commission on Breast Cancer, Transcript of Proceedings, Possible Environmental, April 29, 1993*	*Change class to: HE 20.3152:P 92/5-2/993-4.*
HE 20.3152:P 92/5/993-5	*0507-G-02*	*1994-0400-M*	*President's Cancer Panel Special Commission on Breast Cancer, Transcript of Proceedings, Information Dissemination, June 25, 1993*	*Change class to: HE 20.3152:P 92/5-2/993-5.*
HE 20.3917:200401 1036	*0508-T-04*	*EL only*	*Questions and Answers about Avascular Necrosis*	*Change class to: HE 20.3917:AV 1.*
I 49.89:81/24	*0611-R-01*	*Unknown*	*The Ecology of the Mangroves of South Florida, A Community Profile, 1982*	*Change class to: I 49.2: EC 7/13. Correct item no. 0612.*
I 49.89:81/54	*0611-R-01*	*Unknown*	*The Ecology of the Southern California Coastal Salt Marshes, A Community Profile, 1982*	*Change class to: I 49.2: C 63/6. Correct item no. 0612.*
J 1.8/2: AM 3/TITLE 3/2005/PT.1	*0717-A-01*	*2006-0011-S*	*The Americans With Disabilities Act, Title III Technical Assistance Manual, Covering Public Accommodations and Commercial Facilities, Part 1 of Three Parts, December 2005*	*Change class to: J 1.109/2: AM 3/2/TITLE 3/2005/PT.1. Correct item no. 0717-A-31.*
J 1.8/2:AM 3/TITLE/3/2005 /PT.2	*0717-A-01*	*2006-0011-S*	*The Americans With Disabilities Act, Title III Technical Assistance Manual, Covering Public Accommodations and Commercial Facilities, Part II of Three Parts, December 2005*	*Change class to: J 1.109/2: AM 3/2/TITLE 3/2005/PT.2. Correct item no. 0717-A-31.*
J 1.8/2:AM 3/TITLE 3/2005/PT.3	*0717-A-01*	*2006-0011-S*	*The Americans With Disabilities Act, Title III Technical Assistance Manual, Covering Public Accommodations and Commercial Facilities, Part III of Three Parts, December 2005*	*Change class to: J 1.109/2: AM 3/2/TITLE 3/2005/PT.3. Correct item no. 0717-A-31.*

ANTS-v13-#05-06-05-06/30/06

Classification/Cataloging Update

May-June 2006   2006-03

CLASS	ITEM	SHIPPING LIST #	TITLE	STATUS
J 1.8/2:AM 3/TITLE 2/2005/PT.1	0717-A-01	2006-0011-S	The Americans With Disabilities Act, Title III Technical Assistance Manual, Covering State and Local Government Programs and Services, Part I of Two Parts, December 2005	Change class to: J 1.109/2: AM 3/2/TITLE 2/2005/PT.1. Correct item no. 0717-A-31.
J 1.8/2:AM 3/TITLE 2/2005/PT.2	0717-A-01	2006-0011-S	The Americans With Disabilities Act, Title III Technical Assistance Manual, Covering State and Local Government Programs and Services, Part II of Two Parts, December 2005	Change class to: J 1.109/2: AM 3/2TITLE 2/2005/PT.2. Correct item no. 0717-A-31.
J 23.2:C 79	0208-A-01	EL only	School Vandalism and Break-Ins	Change class to: J 36.15/3:35. Correct item no.0720-C-05.
J 28.2:C 86/2	0718-A	Unknown.	Crime Prevention Through Environmental Design: An Operational Handbook	Change class to: J 28.8:C 86/2.
NAS 1.15:209891	0830-D	2002-0039-M	BOREAS AES Campbell Scientific Surface Meteorological Data	Change class to: NAS 1.15:209891/VOL 117.
NAS 1.26:192272	0830-H-14	1993-1347-M	Flight Validation of a Pulsed Smoke Flow Visualization System	Change class to: NAS 1.26:186026. Correct NASA accession no. N 94-14106.
NAS 1.96:F 64	0830-Z-04	EL only	Mach 3+ NASA/USAF YF-12 Flight Reasearch, 1969-1979	Change class to: NAS 1.21:2001-4525. Correct item no. 0830-I.
T 22.69:V 8/2003	0956-K	2006-0009-E	A Virtual Small Business Workshop CD ROM, A User-Friendly Program to Help You Understand Your Business Tax Issues, September 2003	Change class to: T 22.69:V 81/2003.
TD 4.2:F 26/2	0431-C-08	EL only	Fatdity and Injury Rates for Two Types of Rotocraft Accidents	Change class to: TD 4.210:05/17. Correct item no. 0431-E-04.
TD 4.2:R 27/2	0431-C-08	El only	Reliability of the Gas Supply in the Air Force Emergency Passenger Oxygen System	Change class to: TD 4.210:05/18. Correct item no. 0431-E-04.
X 1.1:107/1-147/PT.8	0993-C	2006-0071-M	Congressional record...Proceedings and Debates of the 107th Congress, 1st Session...Vol. 147-Part 8...June 12, 2001 to June 25, 2001	Change item number to: 0993-A.

ANTS-v13-#05-06-05-06/30/06

Classification/Cataloging Update

May-June 2006   2006-03

CLASS	ITEM	SHIPPING LIST #	TITLE	STATUS
X 1.1:107/1-147/PT.12	0993-C	2006-0073-M	Congressional record...Proceedings and Debates of the 107th Congress, 1st Session...Vol. 147-Part 12...September 6, 2001 to September 25, 2001	Change item number to: 0993-A.
Y 3.C 83/2:2 ST 8	1089-Q-02	EL only	The National Counterintelligence Strategy of the United Sates, March 2005 (Online), Office. National Counterintelligence Executive (ONCIX)	Change class to: Y 3.C 83/2:15/.
Y 4.AP 6/1:SCI 2/2006/PT.3	1011	2006-0155-P	Science, the Departments of State, Justice, and Commerce Related Agencies Appropriations for 2007, Part 3	Change class to: Y 4.AP 6/1:SCI 2/2007/PT.3.
Y 4.AR 5/2 A:2003-2004/3	1012-D-01	2006-0089-M	[H.A.S.C.] National Defense Authorization Act for Fiscal Year 2006, February 16, and March 10, 2005 [H.A.S.C. No. 109-3]	Change class to: Y 4.AR 5/2 A:2005-2006/3.
Y 4.EN 2:S.PRT-107-96	1040-A	2003-0249-P	107-2 S. Prt., Legislative Calendar, 2001-2002, December 31, 2002	Change class to: Y 4.EN 2:S.PRT.107-96.
Y 4.G 74/9:S.HRG.10 8-684	1037-B	2005-0239-M	Buyer Beware: The Danger of Purchasing Pharmaceuticals Over the Internet, June 17 and July 22, 2004 S. Hrg. 108-684	Change class to: Y 4.G 74/7:S.HRG.108-684. Correct item no. 1037-C.
Y 4.G 74/9:S.HRG.10 8-761	1037-B	2005-0239-M	How Saddam Hussein Abused the United Nations Oil-for-Food Program, November 15, 2004 S. Hrg. 108-761	Change item number to: 1037-C.
Y 4.W 36:109-58	1028-A	2006-0162-P	The Social Security Administration's Management of the Ticket to Work Program, March 18, 2004, (Serial No. 108-58)	Change class to: Y 4.W 36:108-58.
Y 4.W 36:108-58	1028-B	Unknown	The Social Security Administration's Management of the Ticket to Work Program, March 18, 2004, (Serial No. 108-58)	Change class to: Y 4.W 36:108-58.

120 Government Documents Librarianship

Update to the List of Classes

May-June 2006		Miscellaneous	2006-03
CLASS	ITEM	TITLE	STATUS
A 1.34/4:	0015	Food Consumption, Prices, and Expenditures (annual)	Cancel class. Now see A 93.64:, item no. 0042-T-12. Libraries selecting 0015 will have 0042-T-12 added to their selection profile. PURL: http://purl.access.gpo.gov/GPOlps3832 (final issue only).
A 13.66/18:	0085-A-01	ECOL Technical Paper	Series title changed to: Technical Paper.
A 13.165/2:	0084-O-01	Annual Northeastern Area Forest Health Protection Insect and Disease Conditions Report	Change title to: Insect and Disease Conditions Report, Northeastern Area (annual).
A 114.1/8:	0034-B-08	Delaware & Maryland Rural Development (annual)	Change format to: (EL). No longer distributed to depository libraries in a tangible format. PURL: http://purl.access.gpo.gov/GPO/LPS60624.
C 3.138/3-4:	0147-B	Current Business Reports, Service Annual Survey	Correction to ANTS-v6-#10-10/31/99. Change format to: (EL). No longer distributed to depository libraries in tangible format. PURL: http://purl.access.gpo.gov/GPO/LPS3529
C 3.138/3-5:	0147-B-01	Current Business Reports, Transportation Annual Survey	Cancel class and item no. Merged with C 3.138/3-4, item no. 0147-B. Libraries selecting 0147-B-01 will have 0147-B added to their item selection profile. PURL: http://purl.access.gpo.gov/GPO/LPS3529
C 3.138/3-6:	0147-B	Current Business Reports, Annual Survey of Communication Services	Cancel class and item no. Merged with: Current Business Reports, Service Annual Survey, C 3.138/3-4, item no. 0147-B. PURL: http://purl.access.gpo.gov/GPO/LPS3529
C 3.158/2-3:	0142-A-02	Current Business Reports, M3-1, Manufacturers' Shipments, Inventories, and Orders	Change title to: Current Business Reports. M3-3, Benchmark Report for Manufacturers' Shipments, Inventories, and Orders.
C 21.12/2:	0257	Index to the United States Patent Classification (USPC) System	Change format to: (EL). No longer distributed to depository libraries in a tangible format. PURL: http://purl.access.gpo.gov/GPO/LPS69299.
D 1.76:	0314-G	Index of Specifications and Standards	Change format to: (EL). PURL: http://purl.access.gpo.gov/GPO/LPS69904.
D 101.136:	0307-A-08	Employee Relations Bulletin (irregular)	Cancel class. Discontinued by agency. Archived issues available at PURL: http://purl.access.gpo.gov/GPO/LPS69086.
D 102.83:	0332-H	Infantry, U.S. Army Magazine	Change format to: (P). Distribution reverts to print format, effective Fall 2003.
D 103.115:	0334-A-02	The Engineer (quarterly)	Change format to: (P) (EL).
D 110.9:	0359-C	Leavenworth Papers	Change format to: (EL). No longer distributed to depository libraries in a tangible format. PURL: http://purl.access.gpo.gov/GPO/LPS71704.
D 110.12:	0359-C	Historical Bibliography (series)	Change format to: (EL). No longer distributed to depository libraries in a tangible format. PURL: http://purl.access.gpo.gov/GPO/LPS58798
D 114.20:	0345-B	Army History: The Professional Bulletin of Army History	Change format to: (P). Change frequency to semiannual.

5

ANTS-v13-#05-06-05-06/30/06

Update to the List of Classes

May-June 2006   Miscellaneous   2006-03

CLASS	ITEM	TITLE	STATUS
D 116.17:	0346-A	CML Army Chemical Review	Change format to: (EL). No longer distributed to depository libraries in a tangible format. PURL: http://purl.access.gpo.gov/GPO/LPS64326
D 209.13:	0419-B	Navy Civil Engineer (quarterly)	Cancel class and item no. Discontinued by agency.
ED 1.45/7:	0461-B-19	Funding YourEducation	Change title to: Funding Education Beyond High School: The Guide to Federal Student Aid. PURL: http://purl.access.gpo.gov/GPO/LPS69761.
ED 1.327:	0461-D-05	Youth Indicators, Trends in the Well-Being of American Youth (triennial)	Change format to: (EL). No longer distributed to depository libraries in a tangible format. PURL: http://purl.access.gpo.gov/GPO/LPS18168.
GS 14.7:	0580-D-02	Joint Financial Management Improvement Program (JFMIP) News	Cancel class and item no. Discontinued by agency.
HE 20.402:C 73/	0497-D-01	TIE Communique	Discontinued by agency.
HE 20.417/2:	0497-D-24	National Household Survey on Drug Abuse: Population Estimates (annual)	Cancel class and item no. Discontinued by agency.
HE 20.3324/2:	0506-A-27	Research Updates in Kidney and Urologic Health	Cancel class and item no. Merge with Kidney Disease Research Updates (HE 20.3324/2-2:), and Urologic Diseases Research Updates (HE 20.3324/2-3:). Libraries selecting 0506-A-27 will have 0506-A-29 and 0506-A-30 added to their item selection profile.
HE 20.4702:R 26/2/	0499-T	Quick Index to General Subjects of Interest Related to Drug Regulation (biennial)	Change title to: Center for Drug Evaluation and Research Reference Guide. Change format to: (EL). No longer distributed to depository libraries in a tangible format. PURL: http://purl.access.gpo.gov/GPO/LPS70223.
I 19.214/2:	0626-C-07	Northern Prairie Publications Database	Correction to ANTS-v10-#02-2/28/03. Libraries selecting 0616-A-03 will have 0626-C-07 added to their item selection profile.
I 20.61/5:	0627-A-04	Division of Energy and Mineral Resources Annual Report	Cancel class and item no. Discontinued by agency with the 1999 issue. Archived copies available at PURL: http://purl.access.gpo.gov/GPO/LPS4074.
J 1.1/6	1063-C	Foreign Claims Settlement Commission of the United States, Annual Report	Change format to: (EL). No longer distributed to depository libraries in a tangible format. PURL: http://purl.access.gpo.gov/GPO/LPS69898 (recent issues); http://purl.access.gpo.gov/GPO/LPS69899 (archived issues).
J 1.14/7-7:	0722-A	Bomb Summary (annual)	Change title to: Bombing Incidents.
L 2.117:	0769-K	News, Employment Cost Index	Change format to: (El). No longer distributed to depository libraries in a tangible format. PURL: http://purl.access.gpo.gov/GPO/LPS1758.
L 2.119:	0769-J	News, Productivity and Costs (quarterly)	Change format to: (EL) only. No longer distributed to depository libraries in a tangible format. PURL: http://purl.access.gpo.gov/GPO/LPS51460.

ANTS-v13-#05-06-05-06/30/06

Update to the List of Classes

May-June 2006		Miscellaneous	2006-03
CLASS	*ITEM*	*TITLE*	*STATUS*
L 38.10/5:2001	*0637-P-02*	*Injury Experience in Metallic Mineral Mining, 2001*	*Correction to ANTS-v11-#6-06/30/04. Correct class is L 38.10:1303 on Shipping List 2003-0148-M. Correct Class should be L 38.10/5:2001.*
LC 1.32/4:	*0785-A-05*	*Federal Library and Information Center Committee, Annual Report*	*Change format to: (EL). No longer distributed to depository libraries in a tangible format. PURL: http://purl.access.gpo.gov/GPO/LPS67435.*
LC 40.10:	*0813-E*	*The Mary Pickford Theater in the Library of Congress [calendar]*	*Change title to: Mary Pickford Theater [schedule]. Change format to: (EL). No longer distributed to depository libraries in a tangible format. PURL: http://purl.access.gpo.gov/GPO/LPS70330.*
NAS 1.1/7:	*0830-C-08*	*Annual Report, National Aeronautics and Space Administration, Aerospace Safety Advisory Panel*	*Change title to: Aerospace Safety Advisory Panel (ASAP), Quarterly Report.*
NS 1.51/2:	*0834-C-04*	*Arctic Research of the United States*	*Change format to: (EL). No longer distributed to depository libraries in a tangible format. PURL: http://purl.access.gpo.gov/GPO/LPS70330*
PREX 2.8/12:	*0853*	*Budget System and Concepts of the United States Government*	*Budget System and Concepts of the United States Government (Dept. ed.), has merged with Analytical Perspectives Budget of the United States Government, (PREX 2.8/5:, item no. 0855-B). Online version still issued individually under current class and item no. PURL: http://purl.access.gpo.gov/GPO/LPS2343*
PREX 2.31:	*0853*	*Mid-Session Review of the Budget (annual)*	*Change format to: (EL). No longer distributed to depository libraries in a tangible format. PURL: http://purl.access.gpo.gov/GPO/LPS2343.*
S 1.30/5:	*0876-B-01 (MF)*	*Ralph J. Bunche, Library of the Department of State, New Acquisitions (annual)*	*Cancel class. Discontinued by agency.*
T 70.24:	*0971-B-04*	*Firearms Commerce in the United States (annual)*	*Cancel class and item no. Discontinued by agency.*
TD 2.2:SI 2/4	*0982-G-05*	*Standard Highway Signs*	*Change format to: (EL). No longer distributed to depository libraries in a tangible format. PURL: http://purl.access.gpo.gov/GPO/LPS70371*
TD 2.8:T 67	*0982-G-02*	*Manual on Uniform Traffic Control Devices for Streets and Highways*	*Change format to: (EL). No longer distributed to depository libraries in a tangible format. PURL: http://purl.access.gpo.gov/GPO/LPS11723.*
TD 2.27:	*0265-F*	*Hydraulic Engineering Circulars (numbered)*	*Change format to: (EL). No longer distributed to depository libraries in a tangible format. PURL: http://www.fhwa.dot.gov/engineering/hydraulics/library_listing.cfm.*
TD 2.30/19:	*0982-G-53*	*FHWA-OP (series)*	*Change title series to: FHWA-HOP.*
TD 12.2:T 68/6	*0982-N-01*	*Transportation Indicators*	*Cancel class. Discontinued by agency with the 2002 issue. PURL: http://purl.access.gpo.gov/GPO/LPS25198.*

ANTS-v13-#05-06-05-06/30/06

Update to the List of Classes

May-June 2006		Miscellaneous	2006-03
CLASS	*ITEM*	*TITLE*	*STATUS*
Y 1.1/5:109-198	*1008-D*	*Water Supply Technology Program Act of 2005, Report 109-198, U.S. Congress 109th Congress, 1st Session, December 8, 2005*	*Omitted from shipping list no. 2006-0072-M.*
Y 3.F 31/8:1-2/	*1061-K*	*FDIC Statistics on Banking (quarterly)*	*Change format to: (EL). No longer distributed to depository libraries in a tangible format. PURL: http://purl.access.gpo.gov/GPO/LPS27481.*
Y 3.F 31/8:1-4/	*1061-K-15*	*FDIC Statistics on Banking (quarterly)*	*Cancel class and item no. Now see Y 3.F 31/8:1-2/; item no. 1061-K.*
Y 4.R 86/1-11:	*1025-C*	*Legislative Calendar (annual)*	*Change title to: Journal and History of Legislation, Committee on Rules (P).*

Update to the List of Classes

May-June 2006		New Item Numbers	2006-03
ITEM	*CLASS*	*TITLE*	*STATUS*
A 13.154/52:	*0015-A-52*	*Lake States Forest Health Watch*	*New class and item no. (EL). Libraries selecting 0015-A-02 will have 0015-A-52 added to their item selection profile. PURL: http://purl.access.gpo.gov/GPO/LPS70928.*
A 13.165/2:	*0084-O-01*	*Annual Northeastern Area Forest Health Protection Insect and Disease Conditions Report*	*New class and item no. (EL). Libraries selecting 0084-O will have 0084-O-01 added to their item selection profile. PURL: http://purl.access.gpo.gov/GPO/LPS70767.*
A 93.64:	*0042-T-12*	*Food Consumption (Per Capita) Data System (updated irregularly)*	*New class and item no. (EL). Continues in part: Food Consumption, Prices, and Expenditures. PURL: http://purl.access.gpo.gov/GPO/LPS35828*
E 10.18:	*0430-Q-05*	*Wind Powering America Fact Sheet Series (EL)*	*New class and item no. (EL) Libraries selecting 0430-Q will have 0430-Q-05 added to their item selection profile.*
ED 1.47/2:	*0455-B-38*	*Education Department General Administrative Regulations, (EDGAR)*	*New class and item no. (EL). Libraries selecting 0455-B-08 will have 0455-B-38 added to their item selection profile. PURL: http://purl.access.gpo.gov/GPO/LPS71039.*
HE 20.427/5INT ERNET	*0497-D-58*	*Mental Health AIDS*	*New class and item no. (EL). Libraries selecting 0497-D-40 will have 0497-D-58 added to their item selection profile. PURL: http://purl.access.gpo.gov/GPO/LPS69475.*

124 Government Documents Librarianship

ANTS-v13-#05-06-05-06/30/06

Update to the List of Classes

May-June 2006		New Item Numbers	2006-03
ITEM	*CLASS*	*TITLE*	*STATUS*
HE 20.3324/2-2:	*0506-A-29*	*Kidney Disease Research Updates (semiannual)*	*New class and item no. (EL). Libraries selecting 0506-A-27 will have 0506-A-29 added to their item selection profile. PURL: http://purl.access.gpo.gov/GPO/LPS69691.*
HE 20.3324/2-3:	*0506-A-30*	*Urologic Diseases Research Updates (semiannual)*	*New class and item no. (EL). Libraries selecting 0506-A-27 will have 0506-A-30 added to their item selection profile. PURL: http://purl.access.gpo.gov/GPO/LPS69694.*
HE 20.4708/2:	*0499-P-03*	*Center for Drug Evaluation and Research Guide, (CDER)*	*New class and item no. (EL). Libraries selecting 0499-P will have 0499-P-03 added to their item selection profile. PURL: http://purl.access.gpo.gov/GPO/LPS70223.*
HE 20.6520/5:	*0491-B-36*	*Guide to Clinical Preventive Services (irregular)*	*New class and item no. (EL). Libraries selecting 0491-B-05 and 0491-B-17 will have 0491-B-36 added to their item selection profile. PURL: http://purl.access.gpo.gov/GPO/LPS68815.*
HE 20.7018/3:	*0505-A-31*	*Trends in Reportable Sexually Transmitted Diseases in the United States (annual)*	*New class and item no. (EL). Libraries selecting 0504 will have 0505-A-31 added to their item selection profile. PURL: http://purl.access.gpo.gov/GPO/LPS67554.*
HE 20.7133:	*0499-F-24*	*AgConnections: Agricultural Safety and Health*	*New class and item no. (EL). Libraries selecting 0499-F-02 will have 0499-F-24 added to their item selection profile. PURL: http://purl.access.gpo.gov/GPO/LPS4*
HE 20.8326:	*0498-C-16*	*Alcohol Policy Information System (online database)*	*New class and item no. (EL). Libraries selecting 0498-C-01 will have 0498-C-16 added to their item selection profile.*
HS 8.8:	*0520-G-04*	*Handbooks, Manuals, and Guides (U.S. Citizenship and Immigration Services)*	*New class and item no. Libraries selecting 0520-G will have 0520-G-04 added to their item selection profile.*
I 1.120:	*0603-B-05*	*Profile (National Business Center)*	*New class and item no. (EL). Libraries selecting 0603 will have 0603-B-05 added to their item selection profile. PURL: http://purl.access.gpo.gov/GPO/LPS66688.*
I 19.53/6:	*0619-E-54*	*Water Science for Schools; La Ciencia del Agua para Escuelas (updated irregularly)*	*New class and item no. (EL). Libraries selecting 0621 will have 0619-E-54 added to their item selection profile. PURLs: http://purl.access.gpo.gov/GPO/LPS66597 [ENG.] http://purl.access.gpo.gov/GPO/LPS67399 [SPAN.].*
J 29.41:	*0717-R-21*	*World Factbook of Criminal Justice Systems (online database)*	*New class and item no. (EL). Libraries selecting 0717-R-01 will have 0717-R-21 added to their item selection profile.*

ANTS-v13-#05-06-05-06/30/06

Update to the List of Classes

May-June 2006		New Item Numbers	2006-03
ITEM	*CLASS*	*TITLE*	*STATUS*
J 38.13:	*0718-H-06*	*Forms*	*New class and item no. (P). Libraries selecting 0718-H will have 0718-H-06 added to their item selection profile.*
L 2.104/2-2:	*0768-D-04*	*Occupational Employment and Wage Estimates (updated irregularly)*	*New class and item no. (EL). Libraries selecting 0768-D-03 will have 0768-D-04 added to their item selection profile. PURL: http://purl.access.gpo.gov/GPO/LPS68663.*
LC 42.16:	*0818-J-02*	*Global Legal Monitor (irregular)*	*New class and item no. (EL). Libraries selecting 0818-J will have 0818-J-02 added to their item selection profile. PURL: http://purl.access.gpo.gov/GPO/LPS70082.*
PREX 28.15:	*0857-T-01*	*Information Sharing Council: General Publications*	*New class and item no. (EL). Libraries selecting 0857-T will have 0857-T-01 added to their item selection profile.*
PREX 28.15/2:	*0857-T-02*	*ISC Document (series)*	*New class and item no. (EL). Libraries selecting 0857-T will have 0857-T-02 added to their item selection profile.*
Y 3.D 36/2:2	*1152*	*General Publications*	*New class and item no. Libraries selecting 1089-R-01 will have 1152 added to their item selection profile.*
Y 3.F 31/8:36/	*1061-K-16*	*FDIC Outlook*	*New class and item no. (EL). Libraries selecting 1061-K will have 1061-K-16 added to their item selection profile. PURL: http://purl.access.gpo.gov/GPO/LPS64511.*
Y 3.H 75/11:	*1018-C-01*	*Legislative Calendar (irregular)*	*New class and item no. (P). Libraries selecting 1018-C will have 1018-C-01 added to their item selection profile.*
Y 3.H 75/11:	*1018-C-02*	*Legislative Calendar (irregular)*	*New class and item no. (MF). Libraries selecting 1018-C will have 1018-C-02 added to their item selection profile.*

126 Government Documents Librarianship

126 Government Documents Librarianship

ANTS-v13-#05-06-05-06/30/06

Whatever Happened To... ???

May-June 2006   2006-03

CLASS	ITEM	TITLE	STATUS
A 13.36/2:R 10-RG-158	0086-C	*Juneau Area Trails Guide, May 1999*	*Reprint of A 13.36/2-6:R 10-RG-125.*
HS 4.106/2:2003/REV.PGS/7	0520-B-09	*Seventh Set of Revised Pages to the 2003 CPB Regulations*	*In 2005 the U.S. Customs and Borders Protection corrected 4-8A-4-8B to 4-8-9 but failed to reflect the change on the cover sheet of the Seventh Set insert pages.*
HE 20.3152:P 92/5-2/992-2	0507-G-02	*President's Cancer Panel Special Commission on Breast Cancer, Transcript of Proceedings, January 11-12, 1993*	*Misprint date on document should read: October 23, 1992.*
J 1.14/7-7:	0722-A	*Bomb Summary (annual)*	*Change title to: Bombing Incidents.*

11

ANTS-v13-#05-06-05-06/30/06

Table of Contents

> *Entries listed in this publication with URLs may have associated*
> *PURLs. To find a PURL, use the PURL Search Form at:*
> *http://www.access.gpo.gov/su_docs/fdlp/tools/purlsear.html*

Administrative Notes Technical Supplement is published in Washington, DC by the Superintendent of Documents,
Government Printing Office, for the staffs of U.S. Federal Depository Libraries. It is published monthly, on the last day
of the month; some months may have additional issues. Postmaster send address changes to: The Editor
Administrative Notes Technical Supplement
U.S. Government Printing Office
Stop IDBS
Washington, DC 20401
Internet access at URL: http://www.access.gpo.gov/su_docs/fdlp/pubs/techsup/index.html
Editor: Laurie Beyer Hall   (202) 512-1114   lhall@gpo.gov

Self-Study Template

The Self-Study is the beginning of the depository inspection process, and while it is likely the inspection process will change in the next few years, some form of the Self-Study will most likely remain. From reviewing the following Self-Study template, you really begin to get a good understanding of what makes a good depository collection and what the FDLP believes to be important. When completing this survey, do not be afraid to toot your horn or explain extenuating circumstances. In my experience, effort counts for a lot with Self-Study reviewers and inspectors. There is also a good FAQ Web page on the Self-Study at www.access.gpo.gov/su_docs/fdlp/selfstudy/ss-faq. html.

Community Served by Your Depository (can be taken from the library's written collection development policy)

Population of the City _____ County _____ SMSA _____
The area's growth can be considered: none _____ low _____
    moderate _____ high _____
Major industries/influences on the local economy:
_____

Types of depository patrons (If an academic depository, include types of community users):

Depository publications most frequently used (If an academic depository, separately include publications used by both community and campus users):

Library's volume count _____ (Includes Federal depository and non-depository materials, all formats, and all collections and libraries under the administrative purview of your library director.)

Does the library have selective housing sites? Yes ____ No ____
If yes, how many? _____
Are Selective Housing Agreements for each in place at the depository,
GPO, and the Regional library?
Yes ____ No ____

1. Collection Development

In this section you will describe the policies and practices that your library uses to build a collection of U.S. Government publications in all media.

1.1 Indicate which statement most closely describes your depository selection.

_____ A comprehensive, retrospective research collection

_____ A blend of current and retrospective holdings

_____ A mostly current, 5-year collection (with a few retrospective holdings)

1.2 Which of the following "Basic Collection" titles does the library select through the depository program? Adjacent to each title, note format received and/or any commercial equivalents. Explain why any are not selected, and where the library can refer patrons for that title.

(Note: This Basic Collection has been updated. See www.access. gpo.gov/su_docs/fdlp/coll-dev/basic-01.html for details.)

Paper	Fiche	CD-ROM	Online	Title, Class No., Item No.
				American Factfinder, C 3.300:, 0154-B-16 (online)
				Ben's Guide to U.S. Government for Kids, GP 3.39:, 0556-C (online)
				Budget of the United States, PREX 2.8:, 0853 or 0853-C
				Catalog of Federal Domestic Assistance, PREX 2.20:, 0853-A-01

				Catalog of U.S. Government Publications, GP 3.88-9:, 0557-F (online)
				Census of Population and Housing (State and County *QuickFacts*), C 3.223/(nos.), 0156-M-(nos),), 0159-B-(nos.),), 0159-C-(nos.)
				Code of Federal Regulations, AE 2.106/3:, 0572-B or 0572-C
				Congressional Directory, Y 4.P93/1:1, 0992
				Congressional Record (daily), X 1.1/A:, 0994-B or 0994-C
				Constitution of the United States of America: Analysis and Interpretation, Y 1.1/3:, 1004-E-01
				County and City Data Book, C 3.134/2:C 82/2/date, 0151 or 0151-D-01
				Economic Indicators, Y 4.EC 7:EC 7, 0997
				Economic Report of the President, PR 43.9:, 0848-F
				Federal Register (daily), AE 2.106:, 0573-C or 573-D
				GPO Access, (online)
				Historical Statistics of the United States * (selected historical statistics) C 3.134/2:H 62/970, 051

				Occupational Outlook Handbook, L 2.3/4:, 0768-C-02
				Public Papers of the President, AE 2.114:, 0574-A
				Sales Product Catalog, GP 3.22/7:, 0552-B-01 (online)
				Slip Laws (Public), AE 2.110:, 0575
				Social Security Handbook, SSA 1.8/3:, 0516-C-01
				STAT-USA (ask librarian for password), C 1.91:, 0128-P (online)
				Statistical Abstract of the United States**, C 3.134:, 0150 or0150-B
				Statutes at Large, AE 2.111:, 0576
				Subject Bibliographies, GP 3.22/2:, 0552-A (online)
				United States Code, Y 1.2/5:, 0991-A or 0991-B
				United States Government Manual, AE 2.108/2:, 0577
				United States Reports, JU 6.8:, 0741
				USA Counties**, C 3.134/6:, 0150-B-01 (CD-ROM)
				Weekly Compilation of Presidential Documents, AE 2.109:, 0577-A (online)

*Title may not be available at all depository libraries as it was distributed in 1976. It can be purchased through the GPO Online Bookstore.

**Copyright restrictions prevent the inclusion of some tables in the electronic versions

1.3   If you do not serve the public as your primary patron, aside from "Basic Collection," what are some of your selections specifically for Congressional District information needs or general public use? (Provide examples)

1.4   Indicate which of the following the library uses:

_____ GPO's Web site

_____ GPO Access

_____ Federal Bulletin Board

_____ Locator Tools & Services

_____ FDLP Desktop

_____ FDLP Electronic Collection

_____ Documents Data Miner

1.5   What FDLP databases and/or publications do you find most useful (Administrative Notes, WEBTech Notes, etc. Be specific)?

1.6   List the most frequently used CD-ROMs selected by your library:

a.   Which are networked?

b.   For which is there access beyond the library?

c.   If no CD-ROMs selected, why?

1.7   Does the library subscribe to any Government online services available through the FDLP? Yes _____ No _____

a.   Which ones? (STAT-USA, Environmental Health Perspectives, NOAA, etc.)

1.8   Indicate which maps your library selects using the following list. Note geographic coverage (county, city, state, etc.) as necessary.

_____USGS

_____NIMA

_____NOAA

_____Forest Service

_____CIA

_____Others

1.9   Does the library have a written depository collection development policy or a government documents component of a general collection development policy? Yes __ No __

a.   If so, attach a copy of the policy, or relevant portions of a library-wide policy, to this self-study.

1. When was it written?

2. When was it last reviewed?

b.   Have you incorporated "FDLP Guidelines on Substituting Electronic for Tangible Versions of Depository Publications" into your written collection development policy? Yes _____ No _____

1.10   Describe any collection development coordination and depository resource sharing efforts that the library attempts with other area depositories in order to eliminate unnecessary item duplication and insure adequate coverage of the area.

1.11   When did the library last conduct a review of items selected? Describe the process. Do you use a zero-based item number selection review? (A zero-based review means "evaluating item numbers on a one-by-one basis [which] should result in adding or deleting items from the selection profile." p. 10, "Collection Development Guidelines")

1.12   Does the library have suitable index tools to effectively access the resources in the documents collection? Yes _____ No _____

a.   If no, what other search tool(s) would you like added to the library?

1.13   Below is a selected listing of government-issued and commercial indices and services. Not all of these tools are appropriate for all types of depositories. Check off the information products and services the library owns. If online access is restricted for some indices, note that fact. Add any relevant titles that the library owns or has access to online.

Paper	Electronic	
		ASI (American Statistics Index)
		ASI on Statistical Universe
		Ames, John G. Comprehensive Index to the Publications of the U.S. Government, 1881-1893
		Guide to U.S. Government Publications

		(formerly Andriot, John. now published by Gale Group)
		CCH Congressional Index
		CIJE (Current Index to Journals in Education)
		CIS Index to Presidential Executive Orders and Proclamations
		CIS Index to U.S. Senate Executive Documents and Reports
		CIS U.S. Government Periodicals Index
		CIS Index to the Code of Federal Regulations
		CIS Federal Register Index
		CIS American Foreign Policy Index
		CIS Index to Publications of the United States Congress
		CIS Congressional Masterfile CD-ROM
		CIS Congressional Universe
		CIS U.S. Serial Set Index
		CIS U.S. Congressional Committee Hearings Index
		CIS U.S. Congressional Committee Prints Index
		CQ Weekly

		Checklist of United States Public Documents, 1789-1909
		Cumulative Subject Index to the Monthly Catalog of U.S. Government Publications, 1900-1971
		Declassified Documents Index
		Dialog
		Documents Catalog, 1893-1940
		EPA Reports Bibliography
		ERIC CD-ROM
		Index Medicus
		Lexis
		Monthly Catalog CD-ROM (What brand?)
		Monthly Catalog, loaded in on-line system, available from OPAC (What brand?)
		NLM MEDLINE
		NTIS Government Reports Announcements and Index
		OCLC
		OCLC FirstSearch
		PAIS
		PAIS CD-ROM

		Poore, Benjamin P. A Descriptive Catalog of the Government Publications of the United States, September 5, 1774-March 4, 1881
		RIE (Resources In Education)
		Westlaw
		Wilsonline
		Uncover
		U.S. Code Congressional and Administrative News

    a.   Other indexes accessible via OPAC:

    b.   Microform collections purchased:

1.14   Who makes item selection decisions for the depository collection?

1.15   Who makes selection decisions for support materials such as indexes?

2. Bibliographic Control

In this section you will describe how the library processes depository materials and maintains a holdings record to the piece level.

2.1   Describe how the library records depository receipts to the required piece-level. Include all tangible information products.

    a.   Monographs

        1.   paper

        2.   microfiche

        3.   CDs, floppies

        4.   vertical file and ephemera

    b.   serials

        1.   paper

        2.   microfiche

        3.   direct mail items

      4.   CDs, floppies

      5.   vertical file and ephemera

   c.   maps

      1.   CIA

      2.   USGS topographic

      3.   other maps (folded map series, NIMA, etc.)

2.2   Is there a significant difference in recording various formats to the piece level?

Yes _____ No _____   If yes, describe.

2.3   Your shelf list for the depository collection is:

_____ card-based

_____ part of an integrated library system

_____ PC-based

_____ other (explain)

2.4   Note any exception to the full check-in record, such as retrospective gaps or materials not usually checked in to the piece level. Note the reasons why the library does not fully record that material. Is record keeping for any material done another way?

2.5   Does the check-in record show library holdings, classification numbers, frequency, location of documents, retention, etc.?

Yes _____ No _____

   a.   If no, what information is not on this record?

2.6   Describe the techniques used to properly identify and date mark all depository materials as required (i.e., stamps, writing on the documents, etc.).

   a.   microfiche envelopes

   b.   direct mail items

   c.   maps

   d.   CD-ROM jewel cases

   e.   floppy disks

   f.   paper monographs and serials, bound and unbound

2.7   List any titles or media that are not marked or stamped.

2.8   Place an example of depository ownership/date stamp in the box. Note the date's significance also, such as date of receipt, processing, shipping list, other.

2.9 Are there processing backlogs? Yes _____ No _____
  a. If so, are these items organized so they can be retrieved quickly for use? Yes _____ No _____
  b. Estimate the processing time for each identified backlog:
    1. unopened boxes
    2. items put in the public catalog
    3. items not entered into the public catalog
    4. continuations ("add ons")
    5. periodicals
    6. microfiche
    7. maps
    8. electronic products

2.10 Is shelving or filing of depository materials completed within 10 days of the date of their receipt in the library (except for items being cataloged)? Yes _____ No _____
  a. If no, how long does it typically take?

2.11 Are at least some documents cataloged and accessible via the library's catalog? Yes _____ No _____
  a. Percentage of documents currently cataloged: _____
  b. Documents have been cataloged since _____
  c. Are you acquiring and cataloging e-documents? Yes _____ No _____
  d. Documents have been retrospectively cataloged: Yes _____ No _____
  e. Plan to catalog retrospective holdings: Yes _____ No _____
  f. Type catalog system used:

_____ Card
_____ Online text-based _____ Web-based _____
Brand of online catalog:_____
_____ CD-ROM
_____ Microfiche

2.12   Does the library subscribe to commercial vendor processing services? Yes _____ No _____
a.   If yes, what services are received, when started, from what vendor, and what is their frequency?
b.   If the library receives catalog record loads, are the records checked against depository receipts?
Yes _____ No _____

2.13   Is the processing of depository receipts integrated into the processing unit for other library materials?
Yes _____ No _____

2.14   To note any missing shipping lists, the library:
_____ keeps shipping lists in order
_____ keeps a shipping list log
_____ keeps shipping lists for (length of time)

2.15   How are missing shipping lists usually obtained?
_____ nearby depository
_____ Regional library
_____ U.S. Fax Watch
_____ contacting LPS
_____ Federal Bulletin Board
_____ not obtained

2.16   Are shipping lists checked against shipments, ensuring that all selected items in that shipment have been received?
Yes _____ No _____

2.17   Are claims regularly made within the 60-day claim limit?
Yes _____ No _____
a.   If no, why not?
b.   Note methods used for claiming to GPO:
_____ Fax
_____ Mail
c.   What percentage of claims are filled?

2.18   Are all SuDocs classification number corrections made routinely and expeditiously?
Yes _____ No _____ N/A _____
a.   If no, why not?

2.19   How is the item selection/deselection history maintained?
_____ Item Cards
_____ Item Lister
_____ Database File
What database file program is used?

2.20   How does the library verify item selections?
_____ Item Cards
_____ Item Lister
_____ Other
_____ Not verified

2.21   Is there a written procedures manual or other appropriate documentation? Yes _____ No _____
a.   If yes, when was it last reviewed or revised?

3. Maintenance

In this section you will describe the policies and practices that your library observes to maintain the depository materials and facilitate physical access for public use.

3.1   Does a written binding policy for documents:
_____ exist and is equal to (or better than) the general library binding policy? Describe.
_____ exist but is inferior to library binding policy? Describe.
_____ exist but is a decision not to bind?
_____ not exist?
_____ exist but not adhered to? Describe non-adherance.

3.2   Does a written replacement policy for lost or damaged documents:
_____ exist, and is equal to (or better than) the library's replacement policy?
_____ exist, but is inferior to the library's replacement policy?
_____ exist, but it is a decision not to replace?
_____ not exist?
_____ exist but not adhered to? Describe non-adherance.

3.3   Explain any strategies used to acquire replacement copies of depository documents, e.g., purchase from GPO, contacting agencies, "Needs & Offers" lists, etc.

3.4   Are depository discards done in conformance with the Instructions to Depository Libraries, the law, and Regional library instructions or submitted to the Library of Congress Exchange and Gift Division? Yes _____ No _____

a. Note the response time for Regional approval.

3.5 The Regional library service for discarding is:

_____ used regularly. Note frequency _____

_____ not used because of lack of staff or time.

_____ not used because library strives for completeness.

_____ not applicable.

If not used, why not?

3.6 Are superseded publications withdrawn according to the Superseded List and "Updates to the Superseded List?"

Yes _____ No _____

a. Are there retention notes on the check-in record that allow for their efficient removal? Yes _____ No _____

b. If retained, are they identified on the spine or cover as superseded?

_____ yes

_____ no, but kept for reference/Regional use

_____ occasionally

_____ not at present

If not, why not?

3.7 Is the depository collection protected from unlawful removal of publications:

_____ as well as (or better than) the rest of the library's collection? State method, e.g., closed stacks, security guard, commercial book detection system, etc.

_____ less well than the rest of the library's collection?

3.8 Does the library consistently remove all packing materials from depository receipts, i.e.:

_____ plastic wrap from paper items?

_____ rubber bands from microfiche?

_____ mailing tubes from maps?

3.9 Does the library routinely update and interfile changes to its loose-leaf depository selections so the material is immediately available for patron use? Yes _____ No _____

a. What resources are allotted to this task?

3.10 Which of the following methods are used to effectively maintain shelves, and to what extent:

	None	Minimal	Moderate	Extensive
Labeled pamphlet boxes				
Notebooks				
String-tied binding				
Vertical file cabinets				
Slotted shelves				

3.11   Are appropriate storage facilities in the library used to pre-
serve depository holdings?
Microfiche metal cabinets Yes _____ No _____
- other - covered acid free Yes _____ No _____
Maps - metal cabinets Yes _____ No _____ N/A _____
- other - covered acid free Yes _____ No _____
Map encapsulation Yes _____ No _____ N/A _____
Archive/"Phase" boxes Yes _____ No _____
CD-ROM metal storage cabinets Yes _____ No _____
- other - covered acid free Yes _____ No _____
Shelves braced if appropriate Yes _____ No _____
Compact shelving Yes _____ No _____

3.12   Indicate the classification system(s) used for all depository
collections in your library and estimate percentages of documents
classified in each classification system:
SuDocs _____%
Library of Congress _____%
Dewey _____%
Other _____%

3.13   What materials, e.g., microfiche, periodicals, reference, etc.,
are integrated into non-SuDocs classifications?

3.14   Are some documents sent to another location, e.g., off site
storage, reference, branch libraries, etc.?

Yes _____ No _____
a.   If yes, where are they housed?
b.   How quickly can they be retrieved?
3.15   Are shelf maintenance policies established and actively followed? Yes _____ No _____
a.   Inventory
1.   Who provides?
2.   How often?
b.   shelf readings
1.   Who provides?
2.   How often?
c.   If no, why not?
3.16   Are documents included in the library's major preservation and restoration activities (e.g., binding, encapsulating, materials moved to climate controlled areas)?
Yes _____ No _____
3.17   Note any major preservation problems (e.g., excessive dust, mold, etc.) and efforts at preserving materials (e.g., spraying for insects, oiling bindings, etc.).
3.18   Does the library have a response plan for disasters?
Yes _____ No _____
a.   If yes, is the depository collection included in the plan? Yes _____ No _____
b.   If yes, is it reviewed regularly? Yes _____ No _____

4. Human Resources
In this section describe staffing levels and responsibilities for the depository collection.
4.1   Has a person been designated to coordinate depository activities? Yes _____ No _____
a.   Is this position currently filled? Yes _____ No _____
b.   If no, why not?
c.   Documents librarian has been in position since _____
d.   Documents coordinator's education:
e.   To whom does this person report?
f.   Hours on reference desk per week:
g.   Hours spent on depository responsibilities:
h.   Does the coordinator also have responsibilities in areas other than Federal Documents? Yes _____ No _____

i. If so, what are the duties and how many hours weekly are devoted to these duties?

4.2 Is there a Documents assistant(s)? Yes _____ No _____

a. Is this position currently filled? Yes _____ No _____

b. Assistant(s) hours a week on depository duties:

c. Has been in this position since _____

d. Hours on reference desk or devoted to other responsibilities per week:

e. Other responsibilities:

4.3 Number of FTE staff devoted to depository operations based on a 40-hour work week:

Librarians _____ Support staff _____ Other (students, volunteers, etc.) _____

4.4 Is the depository operation an independently administered unit? Yes _____ No _____

a. If "No," with which area(s) is documents associated?

_____ Acquisitions

_____ Administration

_____ Cataloging

_____ Reference

_____ Special Collections

_____ Subject Collection (e.g., social sciences)

_____ Other (specify)

4.5 Is there sufficient staff to address basic depository responsibilities? Yes _____ No _____

a. If not, what duties are not being performed and how would a desired increase in staffing aid the depository operation?

4.6 Has depository and/or library staff been cross-trained so that any staff member, if necessary, can do depository technical processing, etc.? Yes _____ No _____

a. If yes, describe:

4.7 Describe on-going efforts to inform public service staff about depository publications, electronic media or related issues affecting service to the depository collection.

4.8 How does the library administration support professional or para-professional staff training, workshops or depository-related meetings?

4.9 Do depository staff members regularly participate in the following activities:

Local depository group (name) Yes _____ No _____When?

State GODORT Yes _____ No _____When?
ALA GODORT Yes _____ No _____When?
GPO Interagency Seminar Yes _____ No _____When?
GPO Federal Depository Conference Yes _____ No _____When?
AALL (American Association of Law Libraries)
Yes _____ No _____When?
Other:

4.10   Noteworthy accomplishments of the documents staff (e.g., conference speaker, committee chair, publications):

5. Physical Facilities
In this section describe the library building and its equipment associated with the U.S. depository collection.

5.1   Indicate which of the following are used in the library:

_____ open stacks

_____ closed stacks

_____ compact shelving

_____ vertical file cabinets

_____ on-site or off-site storage

5.2   Does the library have sufficient shelf, file, and cabinet space to properly house existing depository documents holdings? Yes _____ No _____

a.   If not, explain.

5.3   Assuming continuation of present growth rates, give your best estimate of the depository's growth space, for the following formats (in years):

paper _____

microfiche _____

maps _____

CD-ROM _____

5.4   Does the library meet the requirements for "Public Access to Electronic Information Provided Through Federal Depository Libraries" as announced in Administrative Notes, v. 17, #7, May 15, 1996? Yes _____ No _____

a.   If not, why not?

5.5   Using the following list as a guide, describe the computer equipment available to access the FDLP electronic collection:

a.   Staff personal computers (note general type, number of computers, printers, i.e., 486, Pentium, etc.).

b.   Does the public have unmediated access to the Internet and CDs? Yes _____ No _____

c.   Specify equipment dedicated for depository CD-ROMs and online services and describe work station configurations. Specify RAM capacity, clock speed, microchip class, and type of printer.

d.   Have you used FDLP "Recommended Specifications for Public Access Work Stations in Federal Depository Libraries?" Yes _____ No _____

e.   List other equipment that supports the depository collection, such as microfiche readers and reader/printers, photo-copiers, fax.

5.6   Does the library have a strategic plan for acquiring computer equipment? Yes _____ No _____

a.   If yes, explain.

b.   If yes, will acquired equipment meet the latest recommended specifications for public access work stations? Yes _____ No _____

5.7   Are there stable funding sources for:

a.   computer upgrades? Yes _____ No _____

b.   printers? Yes _____ No _____

5.8   What software is available on public access work stations?

_____ browser (What brand?)

_____ word processor

_____ Adobe Acrobat reader

_____ firewall

5.9   All institutions are required by law to work towards full ADA compliance. Is there handicapped access to all portions of depository collections that are in public areas, including:

_____ ramp(s) or flat entrances into the library?

_____ elevators to all floors housing depository collections?

_____ stack-aisle widths in public areas at least 36" wide?

_____ computer workstations and carrels?

_____ equipment with assistive technologies for the physically challenged? (describe).

5.10   Is there sufficient work space for depository library staff in a non-public area? Yes _____ No _____

5.11   Is patron work space for using the depository collection usually available? Yes _____ No _____

a.   Indicate any times when patron work space is not available near depository collections.

5.12   Are depository operations situated in an environment that facilitates access to and usage of depository resources, in that it is well lighted, climate controlled, ventilated, neat, and clean? Yes _____ No _____

5.13   List any new physical facilities affecting depository operations since the last on-site inspection, including those under construction, or planned for construction. For future projects, note estimated start and completion dates. Describe how these new facilities have affected or will affect depository operations. Types of new facilities could include, but are not limited to:

new library

new addition

remodeling

compact shelving

off-site storage

computer lab

selective housing site

5.14   Indicate which safety mechanisms are permanently installed and fully functioning to protect the depository collection:

_____ smoke detectors

_____ heat detectors

_____ overhead sprinklers

5.15   Describe all types and locations of signs, e.g., library-produced and GPO posters, signs, displays, floor directories, etc., that highlight and direct patrons to depository collections.

5.16   Can a patron unfamiliar with the library easily locate the documents area or documents help desk?

6. Public Service

In this section describe how the library delivers Government information to users.

6.1   Is free and unrestricted access to all depository resources provided to the general public? Yes _____ No _____

a.   If not, explain

6.2   Explain any restrictions on access to the depository collection, e.g.:

Nights

Weekends

Exam periods

Building

ID required

Age

6.3   How many hours per week is the library open?

6.4   How many hours per week is the library's central reference desk staffed?

6.5   If there is a separate service desk for documents, how many hours per week is it staffed?

6.6   Does your library have a written access policy for the depository collection? Yes _____ No _____

a.   If so, attach a copy. Is it consistent with current practices?

6.7   Does the library have a written policy for Internet use that is consistent with GPO guidelines in Administrative Notes, January 15, 1999? Yes _____ No _____

a.   If so, attach a copy.

b.   If not, why not?

6.8   Are written public service guidelines for Government information in electronic formats in place following those published in Administrative Notes, September 15, 1998? Yes _____ No _____

a.   If so, attach a copy.

b.   If not, why not?

6.9   Does the library have any policies and, especially, does it post any signs that may have a "chilling effect" or could be misunderstood by anyone not familiar with the library?

Yes _____ No _____

a.   If so, describe.

6.10   Is the depository emblem posted on or near all entrance doors of the library and selective housing site(s), if applicable?

Yes _____ No _____

a.   If not, explain.

6.11   Does the library offer comparable reference and other services to the "general public" as well as to its primary users (faculty, students, etc.)? Yes _____ No _____

a.   Note any discrepancies, i.e., "priority" services for its own college students, lawyers, etc.

6.12   Describe how the library provides reference services for documents:

_____ A separate reference desk for documents

_____ A combined desk for general reference and documents reference

_____ Multiple subject department reference desk including documents

_____ Other

6.13 Describe levels of expertise of those providing reference service with the depository collection.

6.14 Describe any depository cataloging efforts to enhance access.

   a. Are Federal Government Internet sites included in the library's online catalog?

   b. If there is an online catalog is it networked with other libraries?

   c. Note any other libraries on the network that are depositories.

   d. Does the library's online catalog have dial-in or Internet access?

   e. Is the catalog a shared database with other libraries?

Circulate to:	Primary Clientele		Public	
	Yes	No	Yes	No
Paper				
Microfiche				
CDs				
Maps				

6.15   Circulation of documents is not required. However, for information purposes, indicate which documents may or may not circulate. Explain how a public patron can borrow documents from the library.

6.16   What is the level of staff knowledge of area depositories to make informed referrals?
a.   To what other depositories and for what types of depository materials do staff most often refer users?
b.   What union lists, directories, or area networks are used to make referrals?
6.17   Describe the library's promotional activities for the depository collection and services.
6.18   Does the library have a Web home page?
Yes _____ No _____
a.   If so, provide the URL:
b.   Does it provide links to GPO Access? Yes _____ No _____
c.   To the FDLP Electronic Collection? Yes _____ No _____

7. Cooperative Efforts
In this section describe how the library works with GPO and other depository libraries to ensure the effective functioning of the Federal Depository Library Program.
7.1   How does the depository staff stay knowledgeable of GPO's current guides and manuals?
7.2   Administrative Notes is routed to:
7.3   Technical Supplement is routed to:
7.4   Describe the library's cooperative efforts with other depositories and GPO on the local, state, and national level.
7.5   Describe cooperation with the Regional library.
7.6   Note any depository-specific projects, such as state plans, union lists, etc.
7.7   Is there a local documents group (give group names, acronyms, frequency of meetings, name of newsletter, if any).
7.8   Does the library borrow documents from other libraries for library users? Yes _____ No _____
a.   Is this service available to all user groups?
Yes _____ No _____
7.9   Does the library lend depository documents if requested, either originals or photocopies, on interlibrary loan?

Yes _____ No _____

a. Note any exceptions

7.10 Note any cooperation through electronic discussion lists (e.g., state discussion groups, GOVDOC-L, MAPS-L, LAW-LIB, FEDREF-L, REGIONAL-L, DOCTECH-L, etc.).

7.11 Has this depository assisted or volunteered to help GPO with special projects recently? Yes _____ No _____

a. If yes, describe:

7.12 Is the depository partnering with a Federal agency and GPO to produce permanent public access to electronic Government information? Yes _____ No _____

a. If yes, describe:

7.13 Do depository staff assist members of the general public in borrowing documents from a Regional or another library by:

a. Doing ILL transactions for general public patrons?
Yes _____ No _____

b. Giving citation, referring to public library to complete ILL?
Yes _____ No _____

7.14 Describe how you most often communicate with other depository librarians (e.g., meetings, GOVDOC-L, state electronic discussion group, phone):

7.15 If a problem/question arises with depository operations or depository receipts, who is consulted and by what means (e.g., askLPS, Regional librarian, GPO, GOVDOC-L, state electronic discussion group)?

a. What problems have been addressed?

b. How often are outside resources used?

_____ frequently

_____ occasionally

_____ never

8. Regional Services

If you are a Regional library or a partner in a shared Regional system, fill out this section.

8.1 Explain the Regional's practices on processing weeding lists for its selective depositories. Attach the written guidance given to selectives on weeding, and the frequency of written updates or reminders to selectives about that policy. How frequently are procedures revised? Note normal turnaround times for processing weeding lists from selectives.

8.2   Describe steps taken to implement "FDLP Guidelines on Substituting Electronic for Tangible Versions of Depository Publications." Describe any format substitutions adopted.

8.3   Does the Regional library provide original documents, photocopies, fiche-to-fiche copies on interlibrary loan to libraries in the state or relevant region? Indicate any special materials excepted.

8.4   Describe any consultation services the Regional provides to selective depository libraries under its purview.

8.5   Note any special or routine reference or other service the Regional provides to libraries in the state or relevant region.

8.6   Describe any special or routine visits Regional library staff make to selective depositories under its purview.

8.7   Note any specific assistance offered to depositories with special problems or to depositories placed on probationary status.

8.8   Does the Regional librarian or other staff usually accompany GPO inspectors on some or all of the inspections in their state? Yes _____ No _____

a.   If no, explain why not.

8.9   Does the Regional library maintain files on all depositories under its purview, including such items as GPO Inspection Reports, Self-Study Evaluations and disposal lists? Yes _____ No _____

8.10   Does the Regional library have a microfiche-to-fiche duplicator that can aid selective depositories in interlibrary loan, filling in gaps in microfiche collections, etc.? Yes _____ No _____

8.11   Will the Regional duplicate diskettes? Yes _____ No _____

8.12   Does the Regional have the capability to duplicate CD-ROMs? Yes _____ No _____

8.13   Besides using weeding lists, what other ways does the Regional use to build a comprehensive Regional collection for its state or region?

8.14   Describe how the Regional library takes a leadership role in state-wide Federal depository issues, projects, e.g., new or revised State Plan, union lists, etc.

8.15   Is the Regional library involved with any efforts to provide or ensure permanent access to electronic Government information? Yes _____ No _____

Summary
1. Discuss near-term and long-range goals of the depository operation.
   a. Discuss accomplishments the depository has made since its last inspection.
   b. Discuss how current and projected library budgets may affect the depository operation.
   c. Indicate projects the library is engaged in or plans which will affect the depository operation.
   d. Note any subjective comments about the general direction and progression of the library's depository operation.
2. Add any comments or information that has not been addressed.
3. Attach appropriate items that will be beneficial to the library inspector evaluating your depository operation.
4. Do you wish an on-site inspection regardless of the evaluation of the self-study? Yes _____ No _____
5. I certify that, to the best of my knowledge, the information provided in this self-study is accurate as of this date.

Signatures of:
Depository Coordinator:
Date:
Library Director:
Date:

Bibliography

Adler, Prue. 1998. "'The Times They Are A Changin' For Our Depository Libraries." *Journal of Academic Librarianship* 24 (5): 387–389.

Airoldi, Joan. 2005. "Librarian's Brush with FBI Shapes Her View of the USA Patriot Act." *USA TODAY*, May 17.

Aldrich, Duncan. 1998. "Partners on the Net: FDLP Partnering to Coordinate Remote Access to Internet-Based Government Information." *Government Information Quarterly* 15 (1): 27–38.

Aldrich, Duncan M., Gary Cornwell, and Daniel Barkley. 2000. "Changing Partnerships? Government Documents Departments at the Turn of the Millennium." *Government Information Quarterly* 17 (3): 273–290.

Baldwin, Gil and George Barnum. 2001. "Government Documents for the Ages." *American Libraries* 32 (11): 38.

Barnes, Newkirk. 2006. "Promoting Federal Depository Libraries: Improving Public Access to U.S. Government Information." *The Southeastern Librarian* 54 (1): 20–27.

Beck, Clare. 2006. *The New Woman as Librarian: The Career of Adelaide Hasse.* Lanham, MD: Scarecrow Press.

Cameron, James. "GPO's Living History Adelaide R. Hasse." Available online at www.access.gpo.gov/su_docs/fdlp/history/hasse. html.

Cheney, Debora. 2004. "Government Information Reference Service: New Roles and Models for the Post-Depository Era." *DttP: Documents to the People* 32 (3): 32–37.

Cocklin, John and Linda B. Johnson. 2000. "1999 Bibliography on Documents Librarianship and Government Information." *DttP: Documents to the People* 28 (2): 65–68.

Cross, Barbara Marston and John Richardson, Jr. 1989. "The

Educational Preparation of Government Information Specialists."
Journal of Education for Library and Information Science 30: 28–38.

Depository Library Council. 2003. *Envisioning the Future of Federal Government Information.* Summary of the Spring 2003 Meeting of the Depository Library Council to the Public Printer. Available online at www.access.gpo.gov/su_docs/fdlp/council/Envisioning theFuture.html.

Depository Library Council. 2005. *The Federal Government Information Environment of the 21st Century: Towards a Vision Statement and Plan of Action for Federal Depository Libraries, Discussion Paper.* Available online at www.access.gpo.gov/su_docs/fdlp/pubs/dlc_vision_09_02_2005.pdf.

Depository Library Council. 2004. *Progress Report: How's the Carrot Crop Doing?* Available online at www.access.gpo.gov/su_docs/fdlp/pubs/proceedings/incentives_progress_oct2004.pdf.

Depository Library Council. 2005. *Progress Report 2: The Carrot Crop is Still Growing.* Available online at www.access.gpo.gov/su_docs/fdlp/pubs/proceedings/incentives_progress_oct2005.pdf.

Depository Library Council. 2002. *Responses to Recommendations.* Fall Depository Library Council Meeting, Arlington, Virginia. Available online at www.access.gpo.gov/su_docs/fdlp/council/rfa02.html.

Depository Library Council. 2002. *Responses to Recommendations.* Spring Depository Library Council Meeting, Mobile, Alabama. Available online at www.access.gpo.gov/su_docs/fdlp/council/rsp02.html.

Depository Library Council. 2005. *Toward a Vision of the Government Information Environment of the 21st Century: A Draft Outline.* Available online at www.gpoaccess.gov/images/blog/dlc_vision_outline.pdf.

Depository Library Council. Subcommittee on Attrition and Retention. 2003. *Benefits of Being a Federal Depository Library.* Available online at www.access.gpo.gov/su_docs/fdlp/council/fdlp-benefits.html.

Depository Library Council. Subcommittee on Attrition and Retention. 2002. *Suggested Responses to Frequently Cited Reasons for Leaving the Depository Library System.* Available online at www.access.gpo.gov/su_docs/fdlp/council/soar-suggestions.html.

Dilevko, Juris. 2000. "'My Mother Can't Quite Understand Why I Decided to Go to Library School': What Patrons Say about Library Staff When Asking Government Documents Reference Questions at Depository Libraries." *Journal of Government Information* 27: 299–323.

Downie, Judith A. 2004. "The Current Information Literacy Instruction Environment for Government Documents (pt I)." *DttP: Documents to the People* 32 (2): 36–39.

Downie, Judith A. 2004. "Integrating Government Documents into Information Literacy Instruction, Part II." *DttP: Documents to the People* 32 (4): 17–22.

Drake, Miriam A. 2005. "The Federal Depository Library Program: Safety Net for Access." *SEARCHER: The Magazine for Database Professionals* 13 (1): 46–51.

Ennis, Lisa A. 2003. "Management in the Middle: Life is Unfair." *Info Career Trends.* 1–3.

Ennis, Lisa A. 2003. "Opportunistic Documents Promotion." *Administrative Notes: Newsletter of the FDLP* 24 (7): 25–26.

Ennis, Lisa A. 2003. "Saving a Collection from the Brink of Disaster, Or Life as a Chihuahua in a Rottweiler World." *DttP: Documents to the People* 31 (3/4): 36–37.

Etkin, Cindy. 2005. "Franklin: Your Key to Government Information." Federal Depository Library Conference. Available online at www. access.gpo.gov/su_docs/fdlp/cip/cindy_etkin_franklin_online. pdf.

Federal Depository Library Program. "FDLP Fact Sheet." Available online at www.access.gpo.gov/su_docs/fdlp/libpro.html.

Federal Depository Library Program. 2002. "Federal Depository Library Program Promotion Plan." Available online at www.access.gpo.gov/su_docs/fdlp/pr/promo_plan.pdf.

Fisher, Janet and Tim Byrne. 2005. *FDLP Myths and Monsters.* Presentation at Spring Federal Depository Library Conference and Depository Library Council Meeting. Available online at www.access.gpo.gov/su_docs/fdlp/pubs/proceedings/05spring/ myths_monsters.ppt.

Fletcher, Patricia Diamond. 2003. "Creating the Front Door to Government: A Case Study of the FirstGov Portal." *Library Trends* 52 (2): 268–281.

Gordon, Rachel Singer. 2003. *The Accidental Library Manager*. Medford, NJ: Information Today, Inc.

Government Documents Round Table. American Library Association. GODORT Bylaws. Available online at sunsite.berkeley.edu/GODORT/GODORT_bylaws.html.

Government Documents Round Table. American Library Association. GODORT Government Information Technology Committee E-competencies. Available online at sunsite.berkeley.edu/GODORT/gitco/ecomps.html.

Gordon-Murnane, Laura. 2002. "Digital Government: Digital Tools for the Electronic Dissemination of Government Information." *SEARCHER: The Magazine for Database Professionals* 10 (2): 44–53.

Griffin, Luke. 2002. "Webwatch." *Library Journal* 127 (16): 32–33.

Griffin, Luke A. and Aric G. Ahrens. 2004. "Easy Access, Early Exit?: The Internet and the FDLP." *DttP: Documents to the People* 32 (3): 38–41.

Hathaway, Kathy. 2006. "How the GPO Got Its Groove Back: Government Printing Office and Government Information on the Internet." *The Reference Librarian* 45: 109–128.

Hernon, Peter, Charles R. McClure, and Gary P. Purcell. 1985. *GPO's Depository Library Program: A Descriptive Analysis*. Norwood, NJ: Ablex Publishing Corporation.

Hernon, Peter, Harold C. Relyea, Robert E. Dugan, and Joan F. Cheverie. 2002. *United States Government Information: Policies and Sources*. Westport, CT: Libraries Unlimited.

Jacobs, James A., James R. Jacobs, and Shinjoung Yeo. 2005. "Government Information in the Digital Age: The Once and Future Federal Depository Library Program." *Journal of Academic Librarianship* 32 (3): 198–208.

Jacso, Peter. 2002. "Good and Bad Examples of Government Portals." *Computers in Libraries* 22 (9): 52–54.

Jobe, Margaret M. 2006. "Going Local: Environmental Information on the Internet." *The Reference Librarian* 45: 257–276.

Jorgensen, Jan. 2006. "The Online Government Information Movement: Retracing the Route to DigiGov Through the Federal Documents Collection." *The Reference Librarian* 45: 139–162.

Kawula, John D. and Arlene Weible. 2006. "Catalogs, Indexes, and Full Text Databases: An Integrative Approach to Accessing Government Literature." *The Reference Librarian* 45: 191–206.

Kelly, Melody Specht and Cathy Nelson Hartman. 2006. "The Depository Library Community and Collaborative Participation in E-Government: AskUS (FDLP Librarians) and We Will Answer!" *The Reference Librarian* 45: 19–32.

Kessler, Jr. Ridley R. 1996. "A Brief History of the Federal Depository Library Program: A Personal Perspective." *Journal of Government Information* 23 (4): 369–380.

Kile, Barbara, Ridley R. Kessler, Jr., and Walter Newsome. 2004. "Experience Speaks: Thoughts on Documents Librarianship." *Dttp: Documents to the People* 32 (1): 12–16.

Kling, Jr., Robert E. 1970. *The Government Printing Office*. New York: Praeger.

Kownslar, Edward. 1999. "Closing Down a Government Documents Collection: The Experiences of Millsaps College." *Dttp: Documents to the People* 27 (4): 11–12.

Kram, Lorraine. 1998. "Why Continue to be a Depository Library If It Is All on the Internet Anyway?" *Government Information Quarterly* 15 (1): 57–72.

Kumar, Suhasini L. 2006. "Providing Perpetual Access to Government Information." *The Reference Librarian* 45: 225–232.

Laskowski, Mary Schneider. 2000. "The Impact of Electronic Access to Government Information: What Users and Documents Specialists Think." *Journal of Government Information* 27 (2): 173–185.

LibraryLaw Blog. Possible Elimination of GPO Access Print?: AALL Action Alert. Available online at blog.librarylaw.com/library law/2005/02/possible_elimin.html.

Library Programs Service. Superintendent of Documents. 2003. *Designation Handbook for Federal Depository Libraries*. Washington, DC: U.S. Government Printing Office. Available online at www.access.gpo.gov/su_docs/fdlp/pubs/desig. html.

Library Programs Service. Superintendent of Documents. 1993. *Federal Depository Library Manual*. Washington, DC: U.S. Government Printing Office. Available online at www.access. gpo.gov/su_docs/fdlp/pubs/fdlm/index.html.

Library Programs Service. Superintendent of Documents. 2000. *Instructions to Depository Libraries*. Washington, DC: U.S. Government Printing Office. Available online at www.access. gpo.gov/su_docs/fdlp/pubs/instructions/index.html.

Lyons, Susan. 2006. "Preserving Government Information: Looking Back and Looking Forward." *The Reference Librarian* 45: 207–223.

MacGilvray, Daniel R. A Short History of the GPO. Available online at www.access.gpo.gov/su_docs/fdlp/history/macgilvray.html.

Malone, Chuck. 1998. "Thinking Like a Government Documents Librarian." *Illinois Libraries* 80: 199–203.

Map and Geography Round Table, American Library Association. About MAGERT. Available online at magert.whoi.edu/about. html.

Martorella, Georgina. 2006. "Libraries in the Aftermath of 9/11." *The Reference Librarian* 45: 109–137.

McClure, Charles R. and Peter Hernon. 1983. *Improving the Quality of Reference Service for Government Publications*. Chicago: American Library Association.

McGarr, Sheila M. 1995. "Planning for a Library Inspection." *Administrative Notes* 16 (3): 1–7.

McGarr, Sheila M. 1995. "Snapshots of the Federal Depository Library Program." *Administrative Notes* 15 (11): 6–14. Available online at www.access.gpo.gov/su_docs/fdlp/history/snapshot.html.

McKenzie, Elizabeth M., Robert E. Dugan, and Kristin Djorup. 2000. "Leaving the Federal Depository Library Program." *Journal of Academic Librarianship* 26 (4): 282–285.

Mills, Lois, Larry Romans, and Sandy Peterson. 2002. *A History of the Government Documents Round Table*. Bethesda, MD: LexisNexis Academic & Library Solutions.

Morehead, Joe. 1999. *Introduction to United States Government Information Sources*. 6th Edition. Englewood, CO: Libraries Unlimited, Inc.

Myers, Nan. 2006. "Documents Data Miner: Creating a Paradigm Shift in Government Documents Collection Development and Management." *The Reference Librarian* 45: 163–190.

Nicholson, Andrew, Tom Stave, and Kaiping Zhang. 2006. "Mapping New Horizons in Government Documents Reference Service: A Unique Collaboration." *The Reference Librarian* 45: 95–108.

Nickum, Lisa S. 2006. "Elusive No Longer? Increasing Accessibility to the Federally Funded Technical Report Literature." *The Reference Librarian* 45: 33–51.

Notess, Greg R. 2003. "Government Information on the Internet." *Library Trends* 52 (2): 256–267.

O'Mahony, Daniel P. 1998. "The Federal Depository Library Program in Transition: A Perspective at the Turn of a Century." *Government Information Quarterly* 15 (1): 13–27.

Peterson, Karrie, Elizabeth Cowell, and Jim Jacobs. 2001. "Government Documents at the Crossroads." *American Libraries* 32 (7): 52–55.

Rawan, Atifa. 2003. Virtual Depository: Arizona Project. Proceedings of the Annual Fall Depository Library Conference. Available online at www.access.gpo.gov/su_docs/fdlp/pubs/proceedings/03pro_rawan.ppt.

Rawan, Atifa and Cheryl Knott Malone. 2006. "A Virtual Depository: The Arizona Project." *The Reference Librarian* 45: 5–18.

Robinson, Judith Schiek. 1988. *Tapping the Government Grapevine: The User-Friendly Guide to U.S. Government Information Sources.* Phoenix, AZ: Oryx Press.

Robinson, Judith Schiek. 2004. "We Are All Documents Librarians: Naturalizing the Next Generation." *DttP: Documents to the People* 32 (4): 22–24.

Russell, Judith C. 2004. *Remarks of Superintendent of Documents Judith C. Russell.* Depository Library Council Meeting. Albuquerque, NM.

Salem, Jr., Joseph A. 2006. "The Way We Work Now: A Survey of Reference Service Arrangement in Federal Depository Libraries." *The Reference Librarian* 45: 69–94.

Scheitle, Janet. 2005. Depository Library 301: Electronic Depository Manual. Proceedings of the Annual Fall Depository Library Conference & Council Meeting. Available online at www.access.gpo.gov/su_docs/fdlp/pubs/proceedings/05fall/index.html/janet_scheitle_manual_oct05.ppt.

Schorr, Alan Edward. 1988. *Federal Documents Librarianship, 1879–1987.* Juneau, AK: Denali Press.

Seiss, Judith. 2003. *The Visible Librarian: Asserting Your Value through*

Marketing and Advocacy. Chicago: American Librarian Association. Available online at freegovinfor.info/note/80.

Shaw, James T. 2005. *How to Be a Depository Library without Being a Depository Library: Adding Records for Electronic Government Documents to Our Catalog*. Joint Spring Meeting of the College and University Section and Technical Services Round Table of the Nebraska Library Association, Doane College, Crete, NE.

Shill, Harold B. and Lisa R. Stimatz. 1999. "Government Information in Academic Libraries: New Options for the Electronic Age." *Journal of Academic Librarianship* 25 (2): 94–104.

Shuler, John. 2005. "The Political and Economic Future of Federal Depository Libraries." *Journal of Academic Librarianship* 31 (5): 377–382.

Smith, Diane. 1999. "New Technologies and Old-Fashioned Economics: Creating a Brave New World for U.S. Government Information Distribution and Use." *Journal of Government Information* 26 (1): 21–24.

Smith, Diane H. 1993. *Management of Government Information Resources in Libraries*. Englewood, CO: Libraries Unlimited.

Sternstein, Aliya. Mission Impossible: Printing in the Digital Age, *Federal Computer Week*, January 23, 2006. Available online at www.fcw.com/article92034-01-23-06.

Superintendent of Documents. *Administrative Notes: Newsletter of the Federal Depository Library Program*. Washington, D.C.: U.S. Government Printing Office. Available online at www.access.gpo.gov/su_docs/fdlp/pubs/adnotes/index.html.

Superintendent of Documents. *Keeping America Informed: Federal Depository Library Program*. Washington, D.C.: U.S. Government Printing Office. Available online at www.access.gpo.gov/su_docs/fdlp/pr/keepam.html.

Superintendent of Documents. 2005. *Policy Statement: Dissemination/Distribution Policy for the Federal Depository Library Program*. Washington, D.C.: U.S. Government Printing Office.

Tipton, Jocelyn T. 2006. "Government Statistical Data: Changes Impacting Access and Service." *The Reference Librarian* 45: 53–67.

"Title 44—Public Printing and Documents Chapter 19—Depository Library Program," U.S. Code Online. Available online at www.access.gpo.gov/su_docs/dpos/title44.html.

U.S. Government Printing Office. 2005 Biennial Survey of Depository Libraries. Available online at www.access.gpo.gov/su_docs/ fdlp/bisurvey/05bsq-final.pdf.

U.S. Government Printing Office. Federal Depository Library Program. *The Electronic Federal Depository Library Manual.* Available online at (unpublished).

U.S. Government Printing Office. Library Programs Service. *FY 2002 Annual Report.* Available online at www.access.gpo.gov/su_ docs/fdlp/pubs/annrprt/02lpsar.html.

U.S. Government Printing Office. Office of Information Dissemination. 2005. *Information Dissemination Implementation Plan, FY 2005–2006.* Washington, D.C.: U.S. Government Printing Office.

U.S. Government Printing Office. 2004. *Annual Report: Leading Our Customers into the Digital Future.* Available online at www.gpo.gov/congressional/annualreports/04annrep/GPO_2004 _ANNUAL_REPORT_web.pdf.

U.S. Government Printing Office. 2005. *Annual Report: Voices of Change.* Available online at a257.g.akamaitech.net/7/257/ 2422/17jan20061430/www.gpo.gov/congressional/annual reports/05annrep/GPOAnnualReport2005.pdf.

U.S. Government Printing Office. 2004. *Bruce R. James Public Printer of the United States Prepared Statement before the Committee on House Administration U.S. House of Representatives on the Transformation of the U.S. Government Printing Office to Meet the Demands of the 21st Century.* Available online at appropriations. senate.gov/hearmarkups/record.cfm?id=218689.

U.S. Government Printing Office. "Depository Library Council: About." Available online at www.access.gpo.gov/su_docs/ fdlp/council/aboutdlc.html.

U.S. Government Printing Office. 2005. "Depository Library Council Meeting Update." Available online at www.access.gpo.gov/ su_docs/fdlp/pubs/adnotes/ad09_10_1505.html#4.

U.S. Government Printing Office, "Future Digital System (FDsys)." Available online at www.gpo.gov/projects/fdsys.htm.

U.S. Government Printing Office. *GPO Frequently Asked Questions.* Available at www.gpo.gov/factsheet/index.html.

U.S. Government Printing Office. 2005. *GPO's Digital Content System: Update for the Fall Conference of the Depository Library Council.* Available online at www.access.gpo.gov/ su_docs/fdlp/pubs/ proceedings/05fall/mike_wash_fdsys_oct05.pdf.

U.S. Government Printing Office. LOCKSS Pilot Project. Available online at www.access.gpo.gov/su_docs/fdlp/lockss/.

U.S. Government Printing Office. "Permanent Public Access Working Group to U.S. Government Information." Available online at www.gpo.gov/ppa/index.html

U.S. Government Printing Office. 2005. "Plenary Session on Strategic Vision and GPO's Future Digital System: Phase 3." Available online at www.access.gpo.gov/su_docs/fdlp/pubs/proceedings/05spring/ cdqa/bj_mw_cdqa.pdf.

U.S. Government Printing Office. Proceedings of the Ninth Annual Federal Depository Conference. Available online at www.access. gpo.gov/su_docs/fdlp/pubs/proceedings/00proa.html.

U.S. Government Printing Office. Self-Study of a Federal Depository Library. Available online at www.access.gpo.gov/su_docs/fdlp/ pubs/fdlm/selfstud.html.

U.S. Government Printing Office. 2004. *A Strategic Vision for the 21st Century.* Available online at www.gpo.gov/congressional/pdfs/ 04strategicplan.pdf.

Weatherly, C. Diann. 1996. "A U.S. Government Publications Collection in a Non-Depository Research Library: A Case Study." *Journal of Government Information* 23 (4): 471–489.

Weatherly, C. Diann. 1997. *To Be or Not to Be a Depository: Answering the Questions and Envisioning a Brighter Future.* Proceedings of the 6th Annual Federal Depository Library Conference.

Wilhite, Jeffrey M. 2004. "Internet Versus Live: Assessment of Government Documents Bibliographic Instruction." *Journal of Government Information* 30 (5): 561–574.

Wilhite, Jeffrey M. 1998. "The Road to Service Standards in a Government Documents Collection: The Methodology of Surveying." *Journal of Government Information* 25 (3): 285–297.

Yang, Zheng Ye (Lan). 2001. "An Assessment of Education and Training Needs for Government Documents Librarians in the United States." *Journal of Government Information* 28 (4): 425–439.

About the Author

Lisa Ennis is currently the systems librarian at the Lister Hill Library of the Health Sciences at the University of Alabama at Birmingham. Before moving to Birmingham, Lisa was the government documents librarian at Georgia College & State University. She received her BA in history from Mercer University in Macon, Georgia, an MA in history from Georgia College & State University, and her MS in Information Science from the University of Tennessee. She has published several articles on numerous library topics including digital reference, management, and technostress. Lisa is also a regular reviewer for the *Library Journal* as well as other publications. She is currently working on a project researching leadership qualities and characteristics of library directors. In addition to her library publications, Lisa also enjoys publishing in social history, especially women's sports and the history of medicine. She also finds time to play with her dog, Gracie, and grow tomatoes. She can be contacted at lennis@uab.edu.

Index

A

AALL (American Association of Law Libraries), 44

access
to electronic materials, 22, 23–24, 65–67
goals, 65
to medical information, 66
physical limitations, 58, 63
policy for, 55
requirements, 61–62, 65, 66
studies on, 23
to tangible materials, 62–65

Access Policy, 55

administration activities, 51

Ahrens, Aric G., 23, 31

ALA (American Library Association), 5, 43, 44. *See also* GODORT

American Association of Law Libraries (AALL), 44

American Library Association (ALA), 5, 43, 44. *See also* GODORT

Americans with Disabilities Act, 58

Annual Item Selection Cycle, 77

Antiquarian Society of Worchester, Massachusetts, 13

"Ask a Question" Web form, GPO, 48

Association of Research Libraries research study, 23

authentication, document, 82–83

B

Baldwin, Gil, 25

barcodes, 80, 81

Barnum, George, 25

Biennial Survey (FDLP), 15, 54

Binding Policy, 55, 81

Blattenberger, Raymond, 12

blogs, 47–48

books on government documents, 49

"A Brief History of the Federal Depository Program: A Personal Perspective" (Kessler), 13

Bullock Perfecting Press, 10

buy-in, interdepartmental, 52

C

cataloging, 6, 79–80, 81

Catalog of U.S. Government Publications, 77

CD-ROM materials, 22, 64

censorship, online information, 66

Cheverie, Joan F., 49

circulation rules, 62. *See also* access

Civil War, GPO role in, 10

classification, document, 10, 57, 78–79

"Classified List of United States Publications", 14–15

"Closing Down a Government Documents Collection: The Experiences of Millsaps College" (Kownslar), 37–38